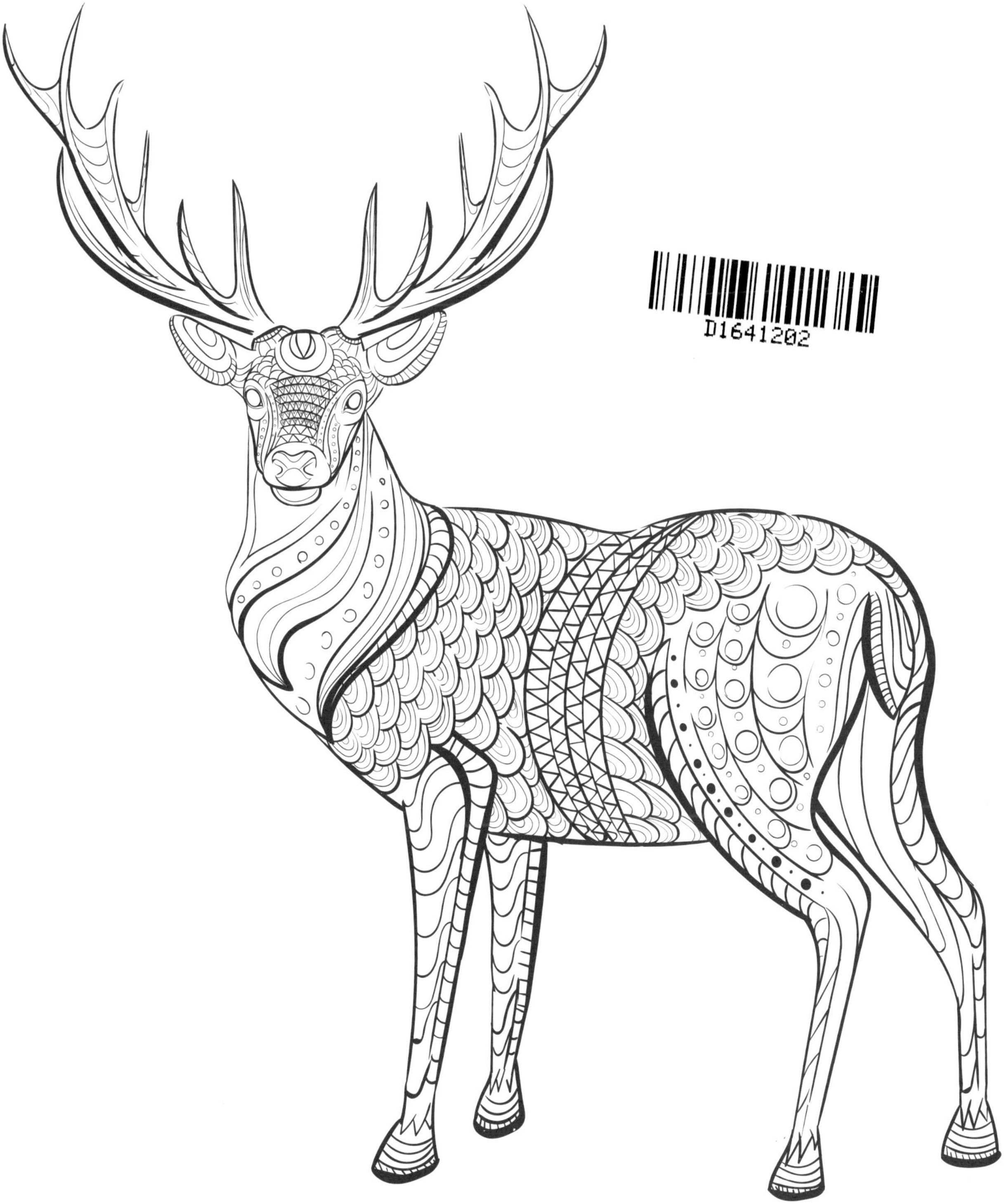

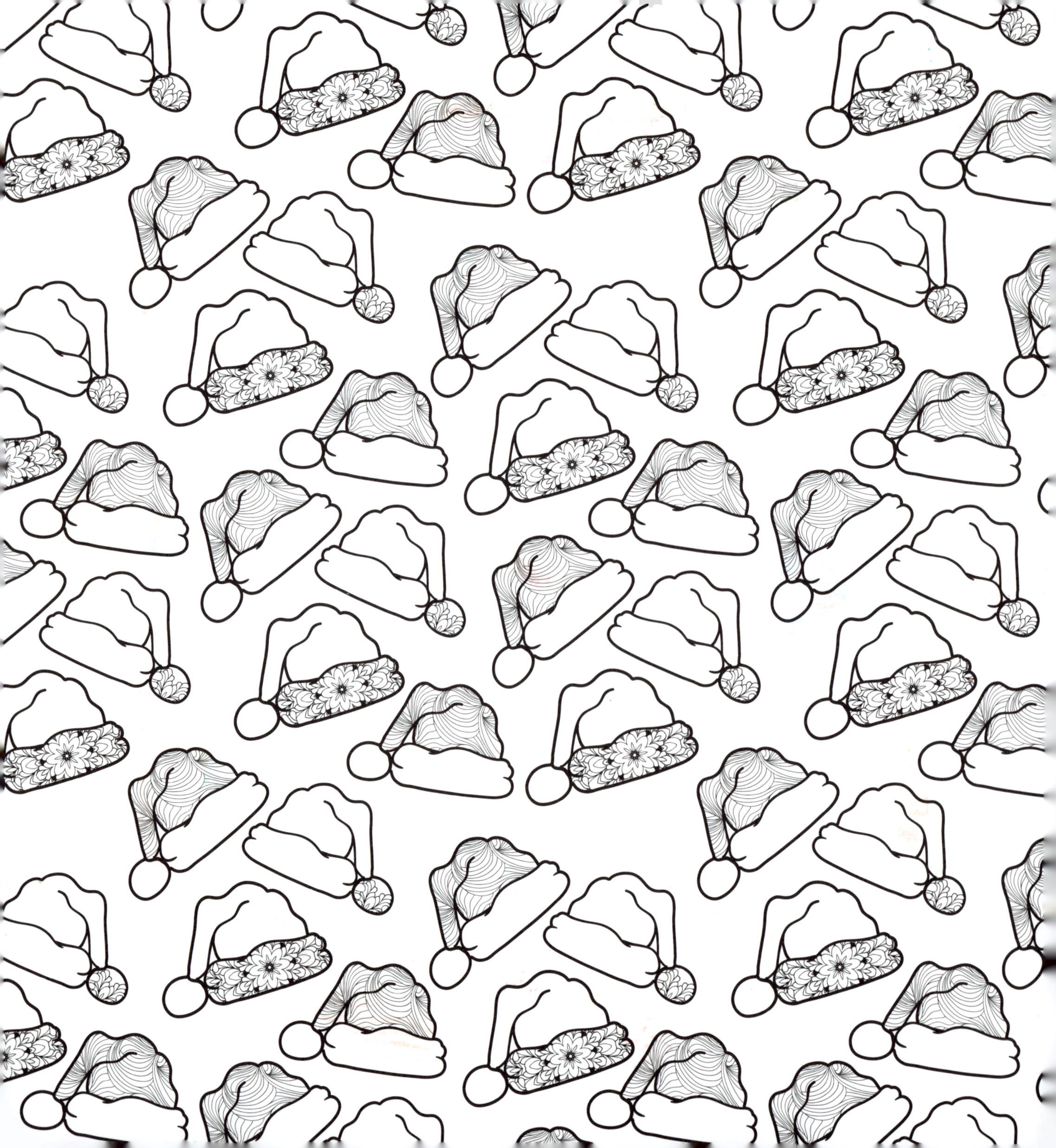

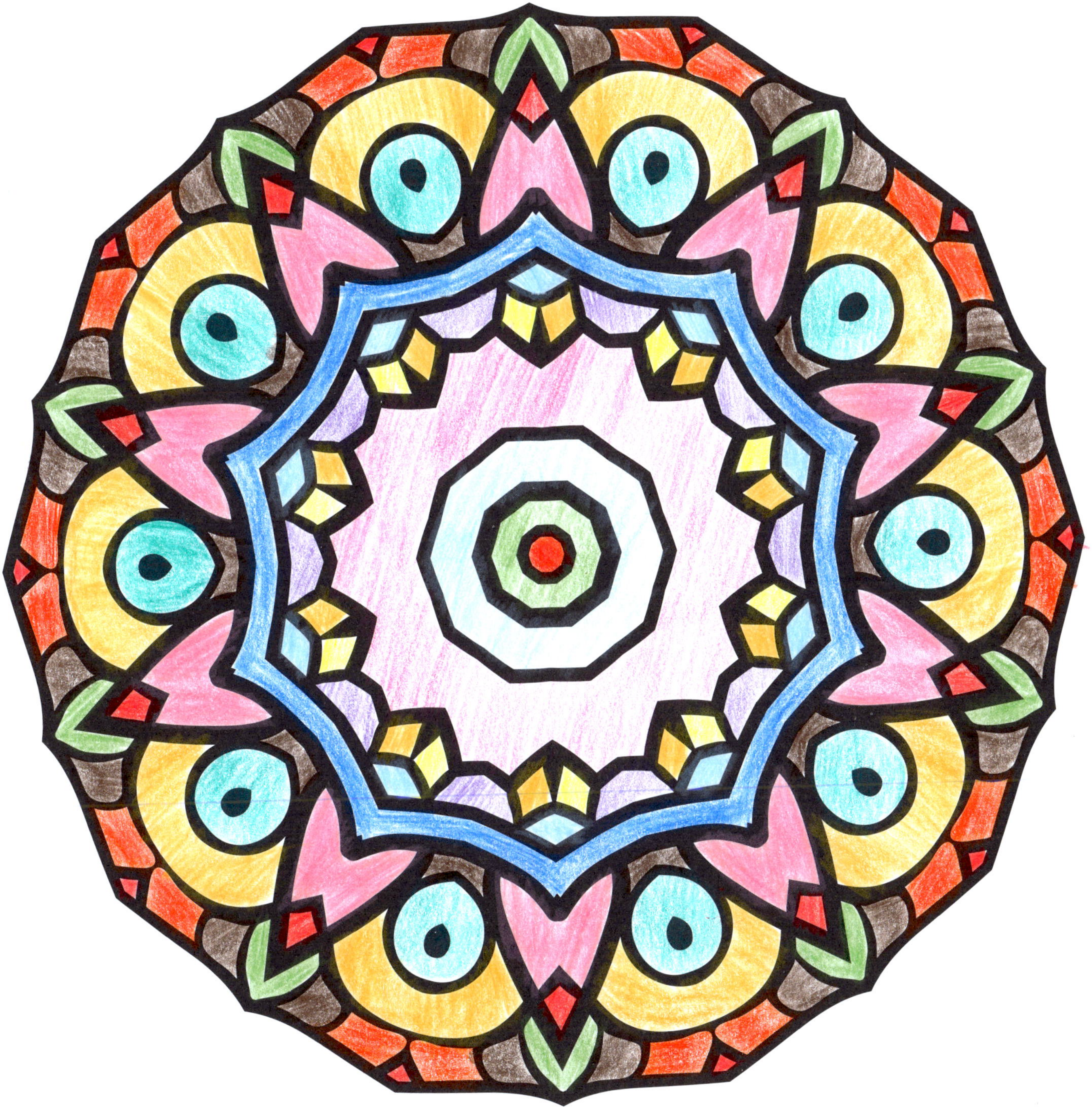

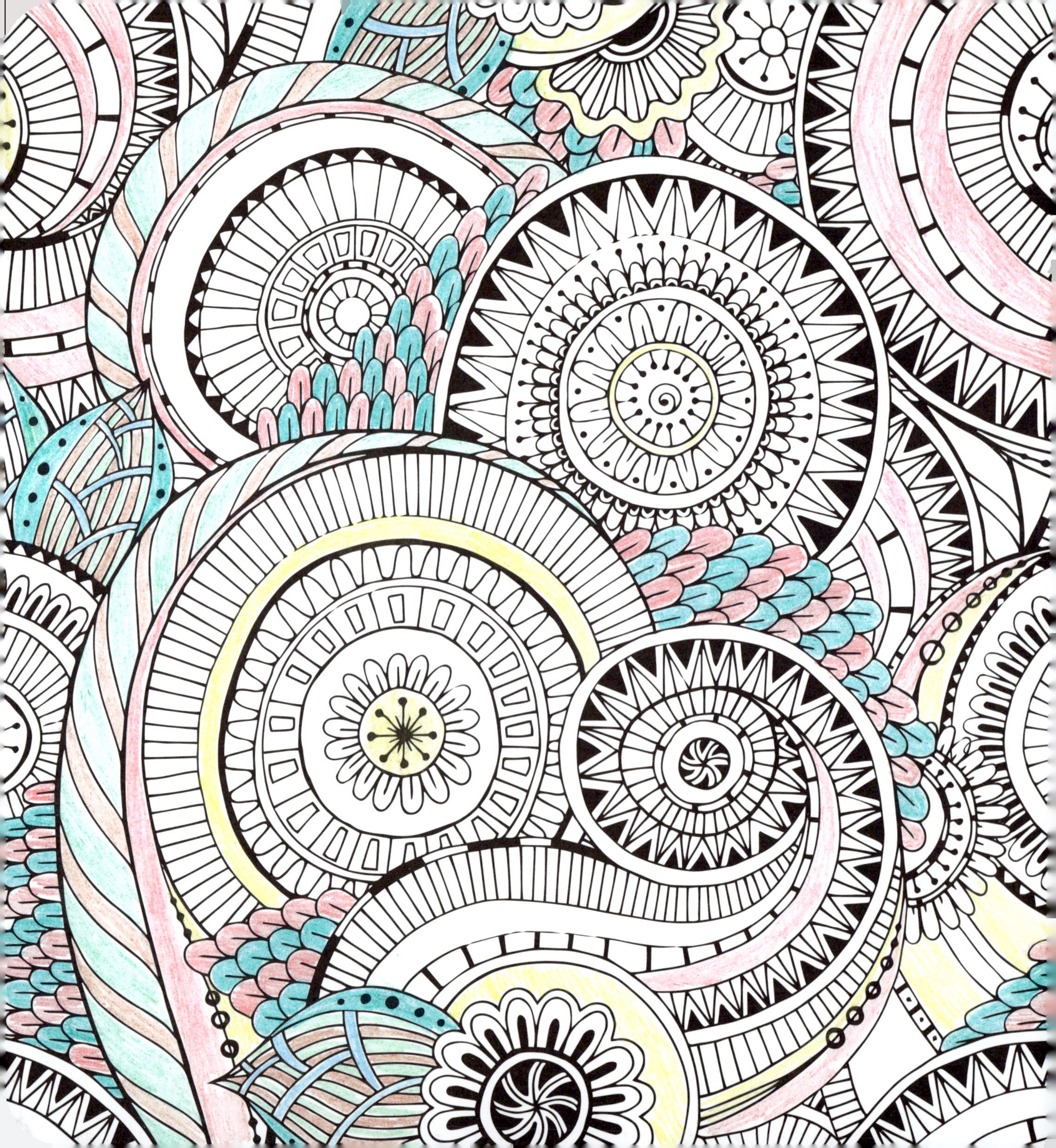

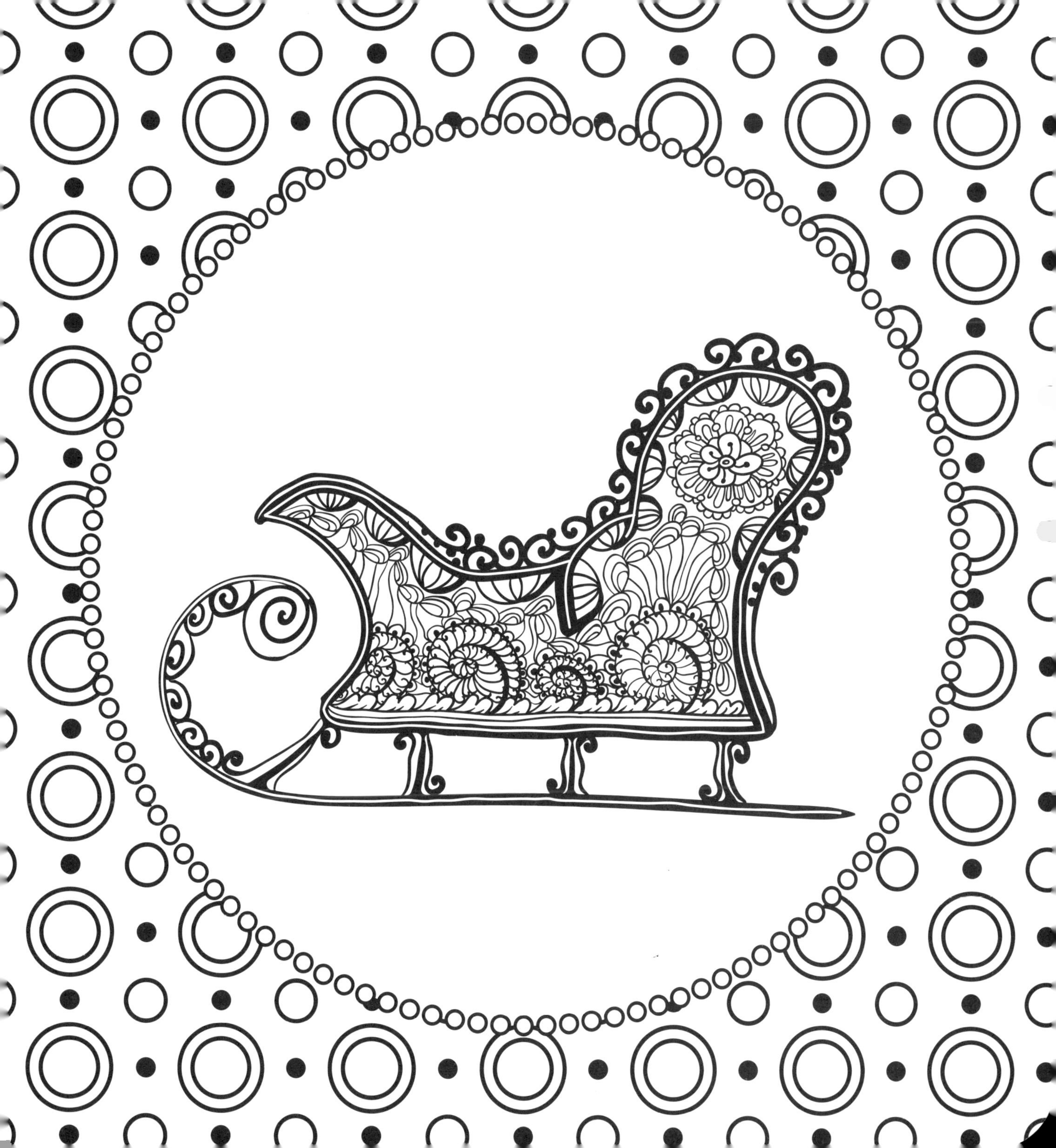

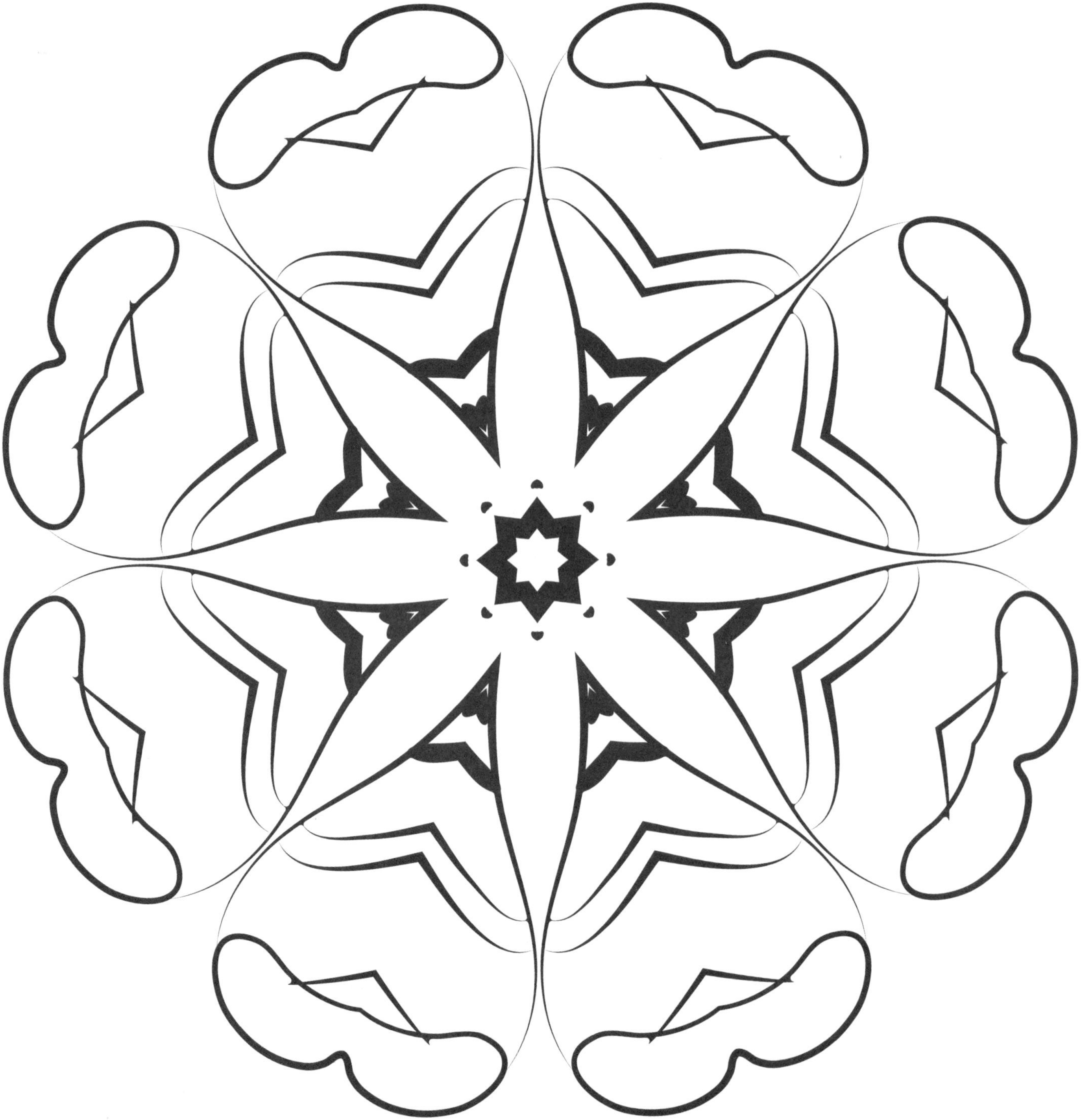

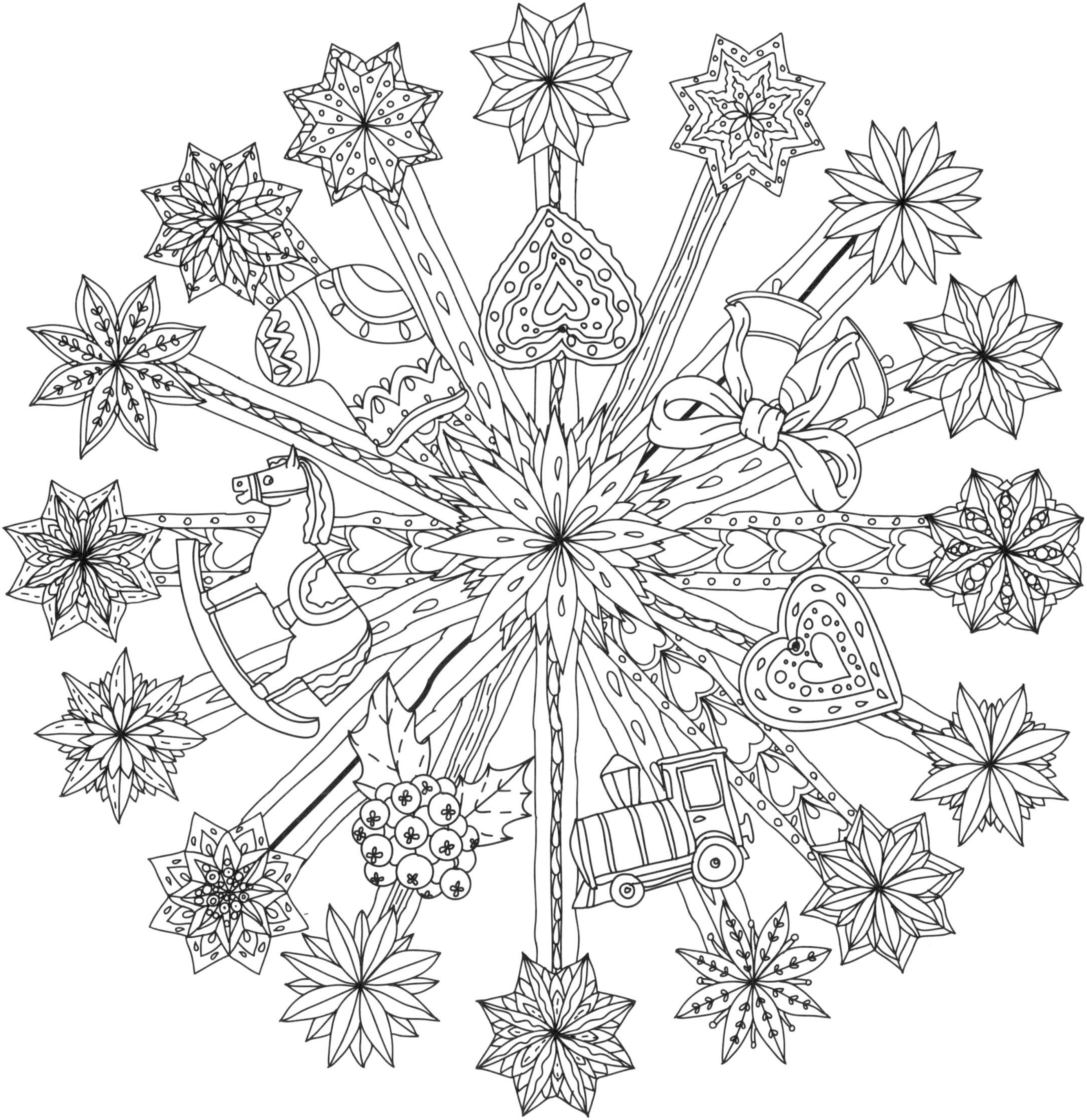

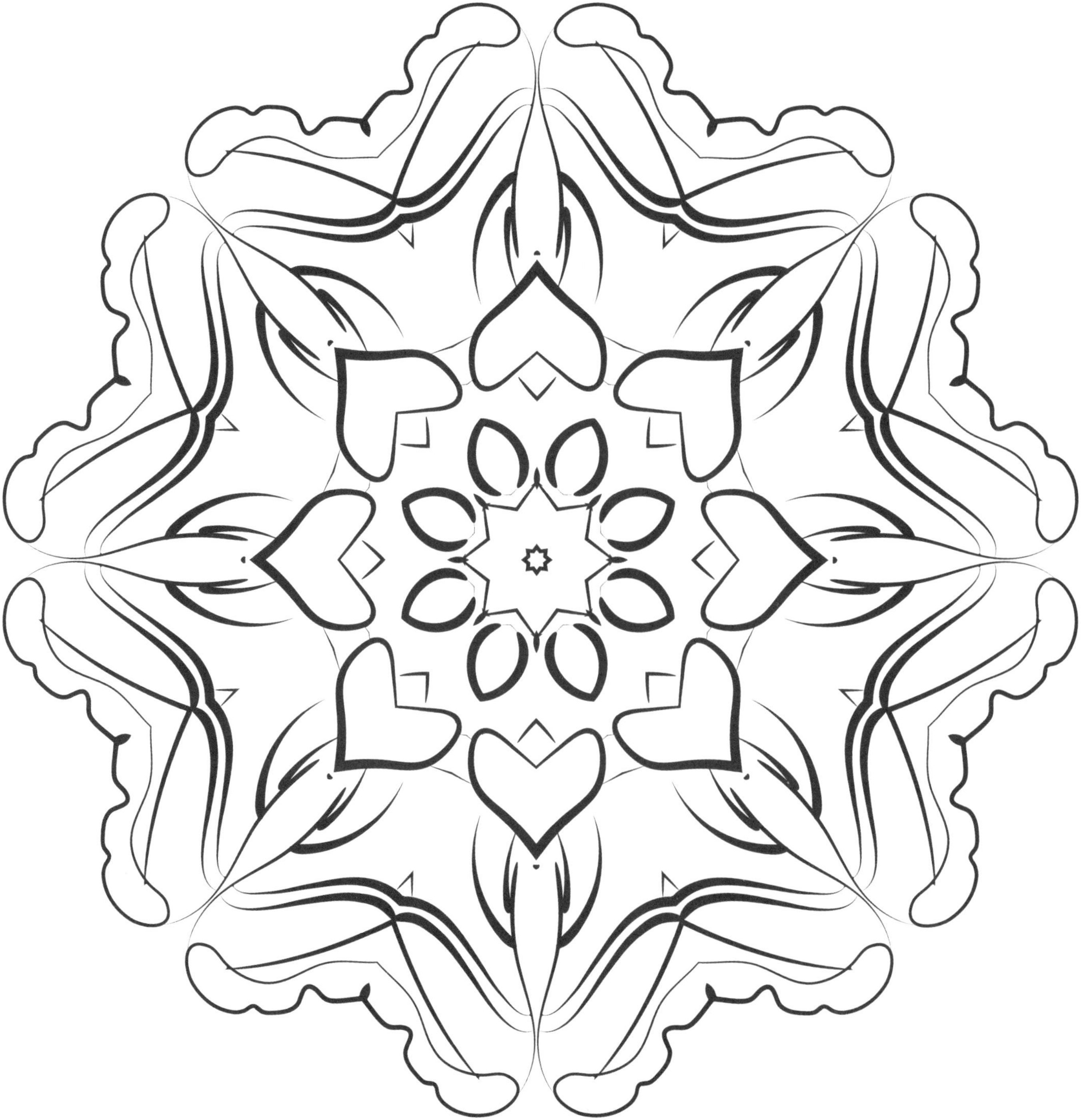

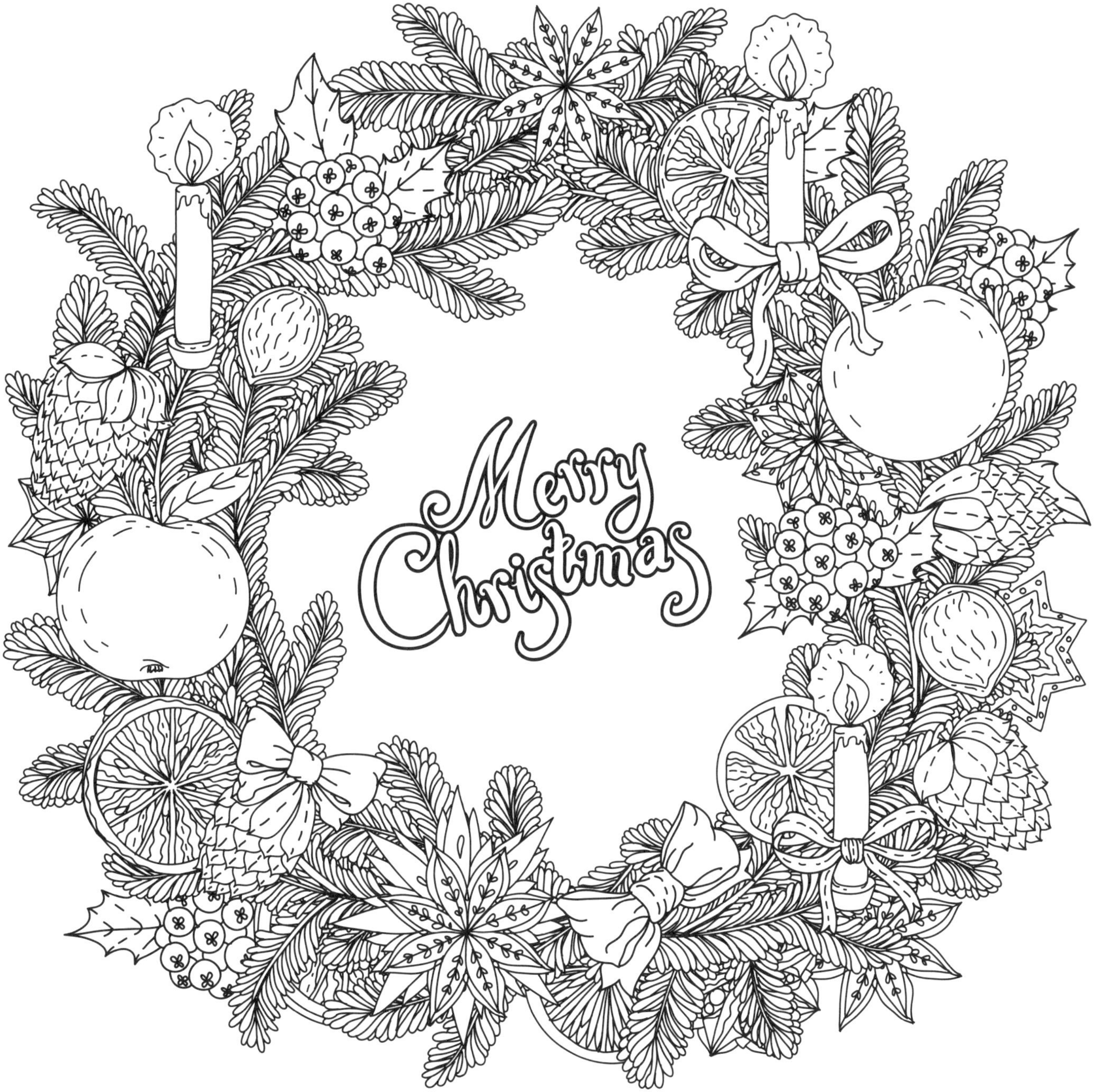
Merry Christmas

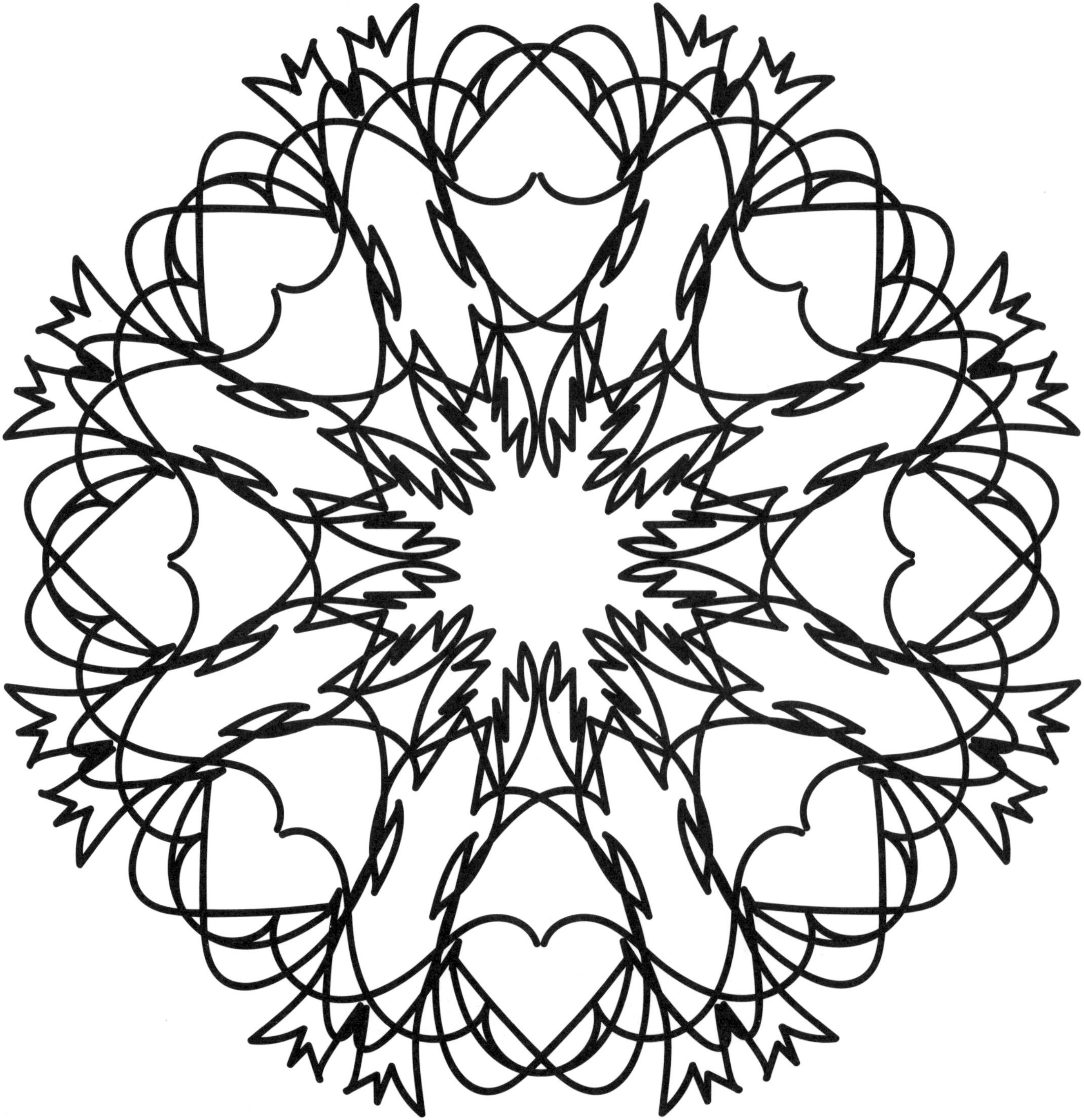

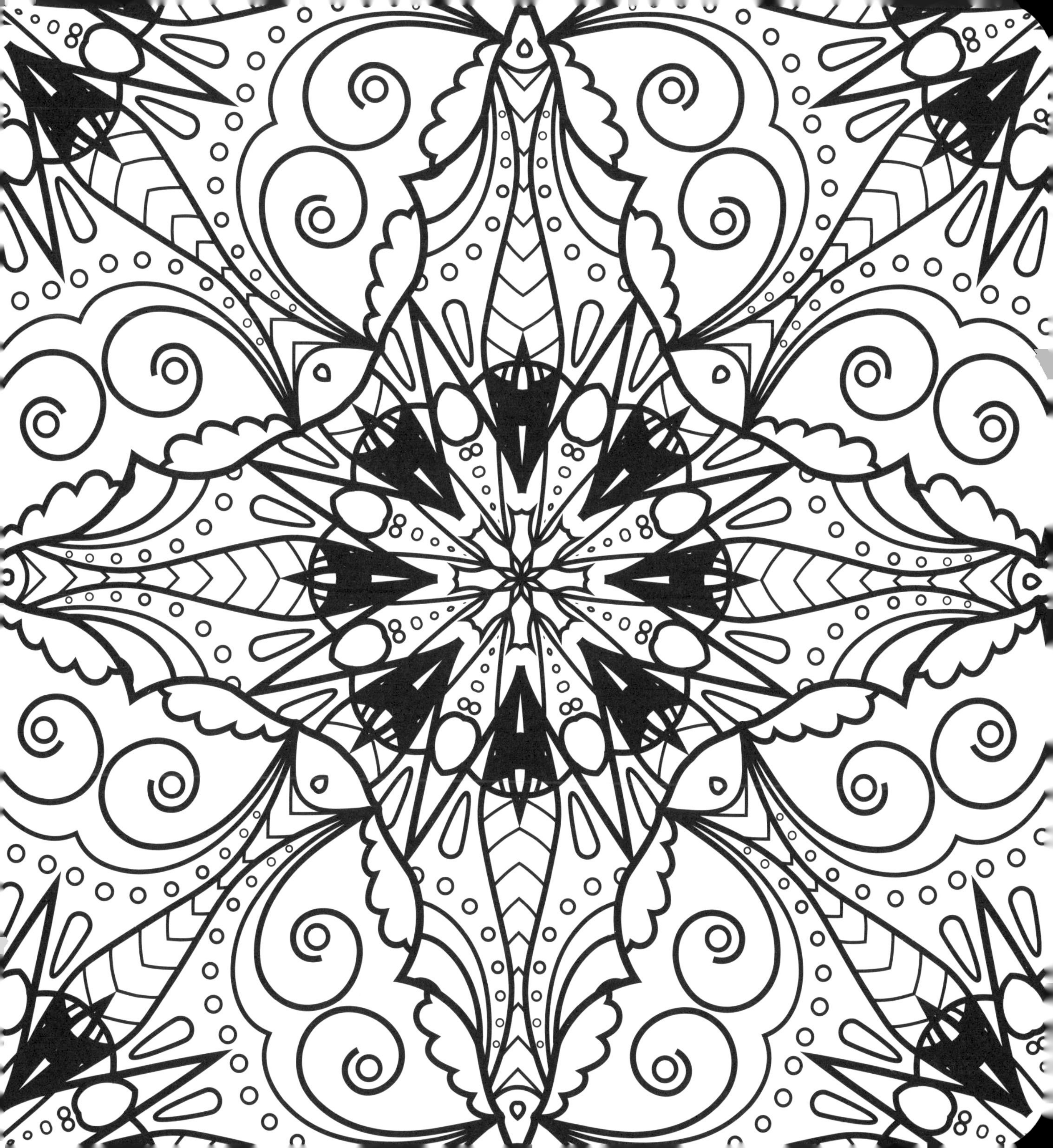

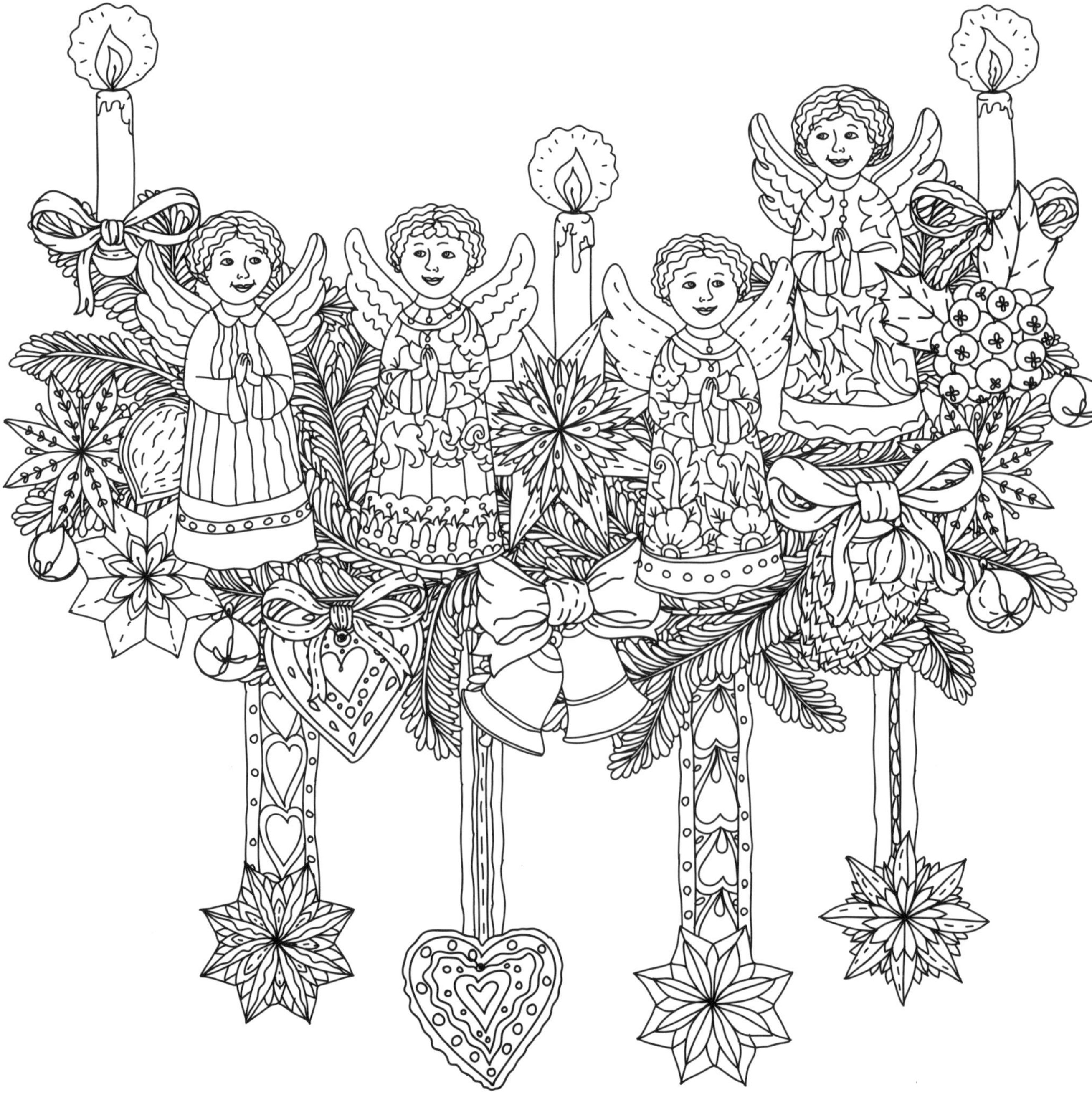

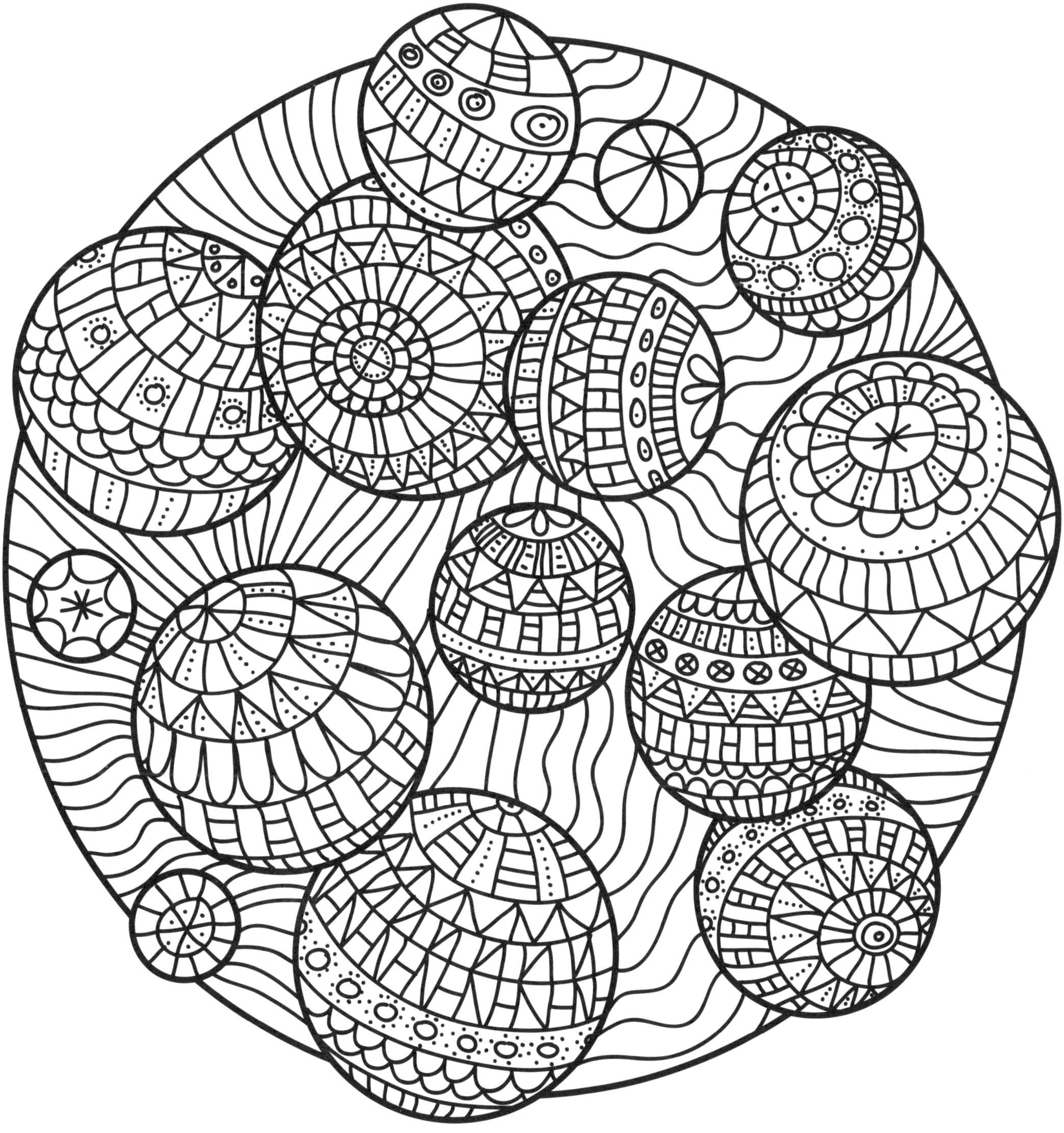

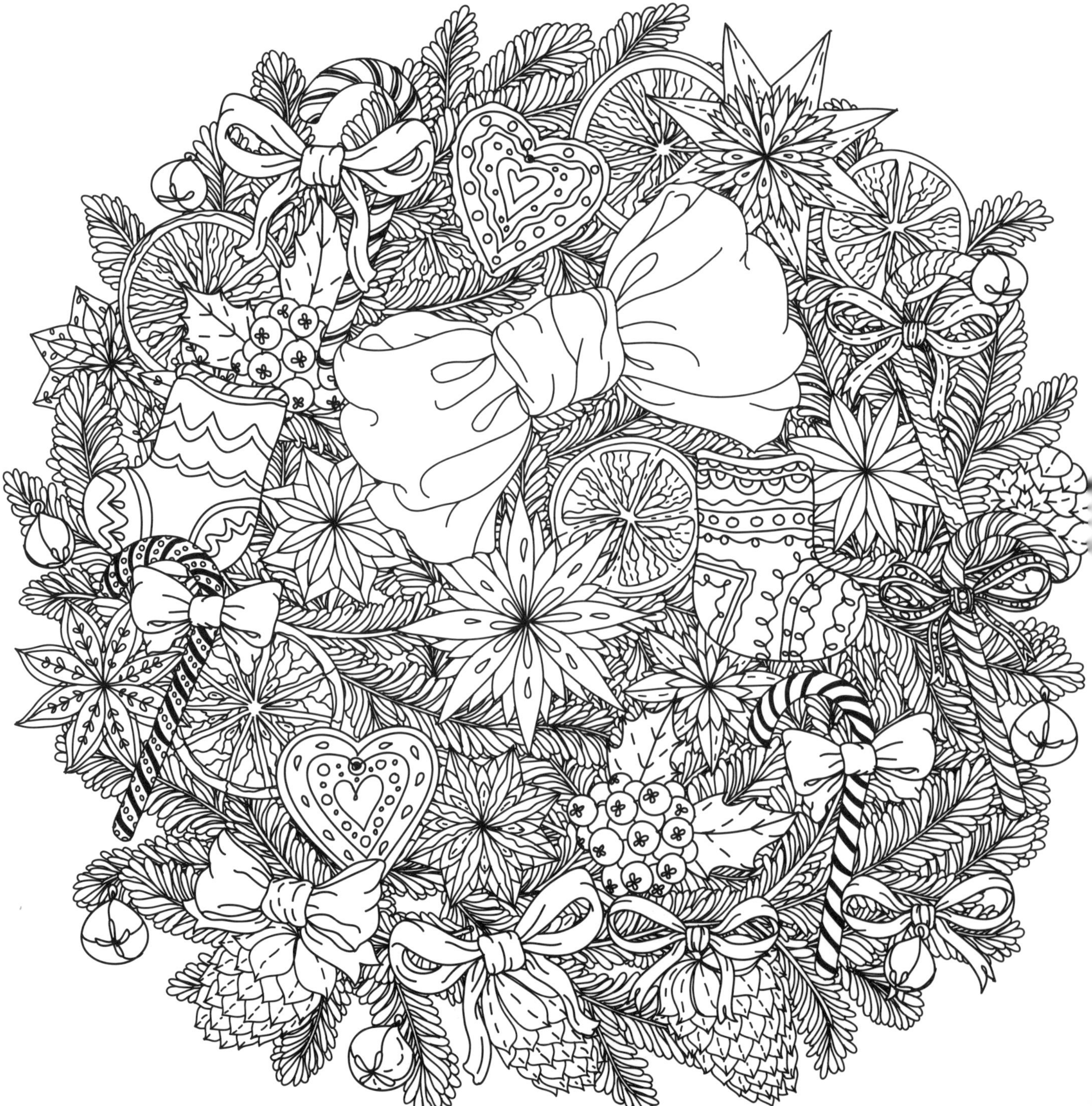

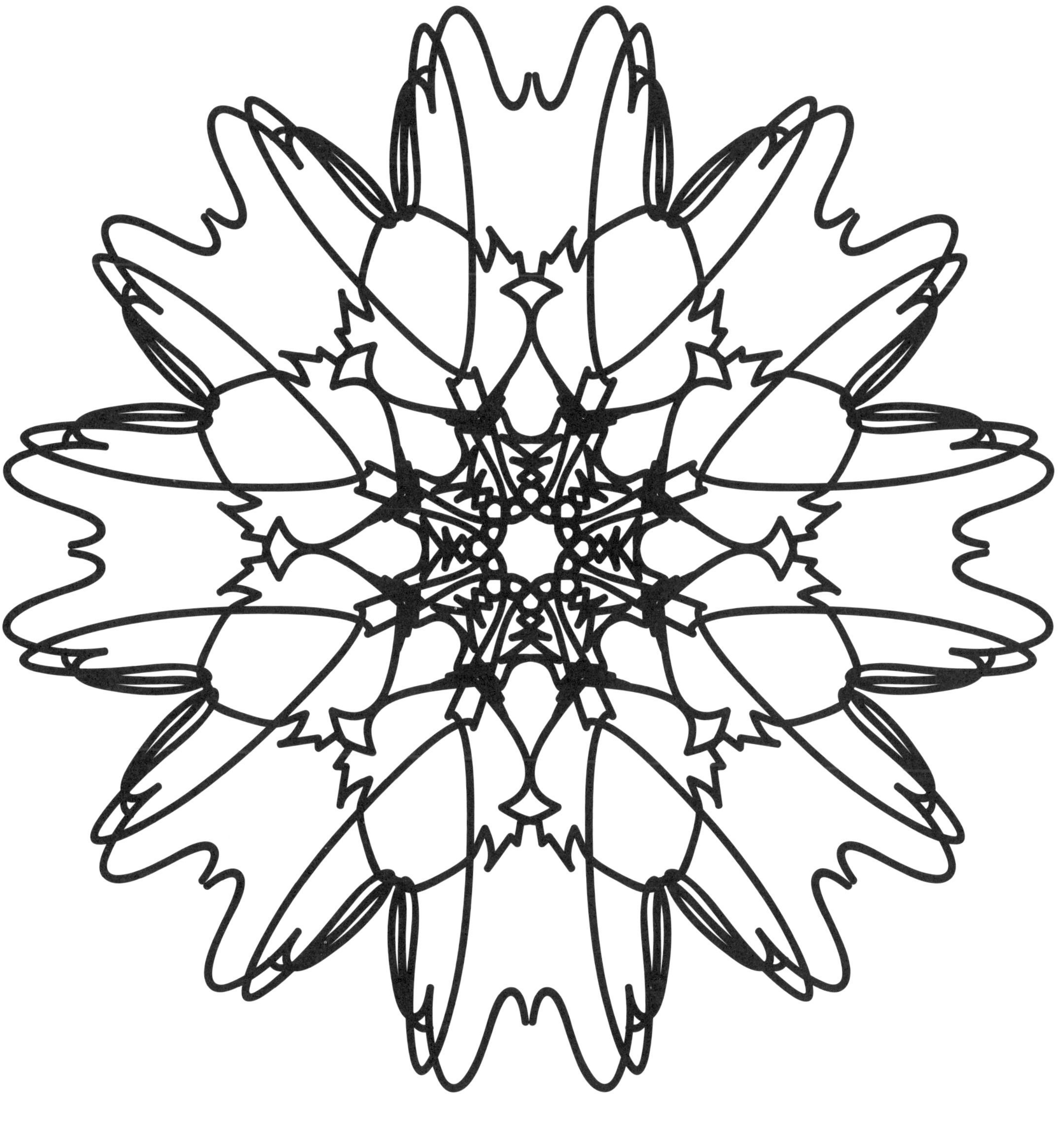

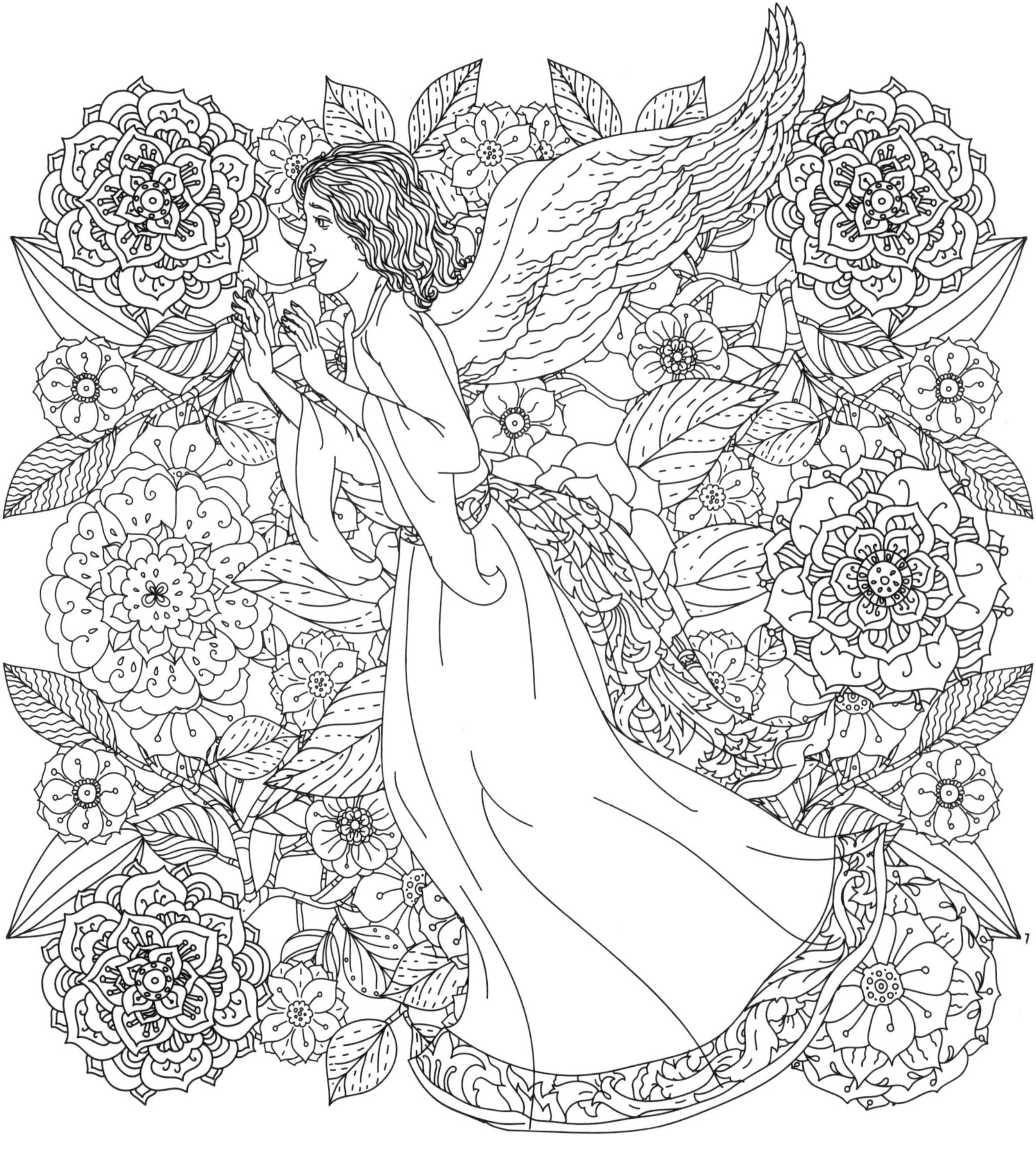

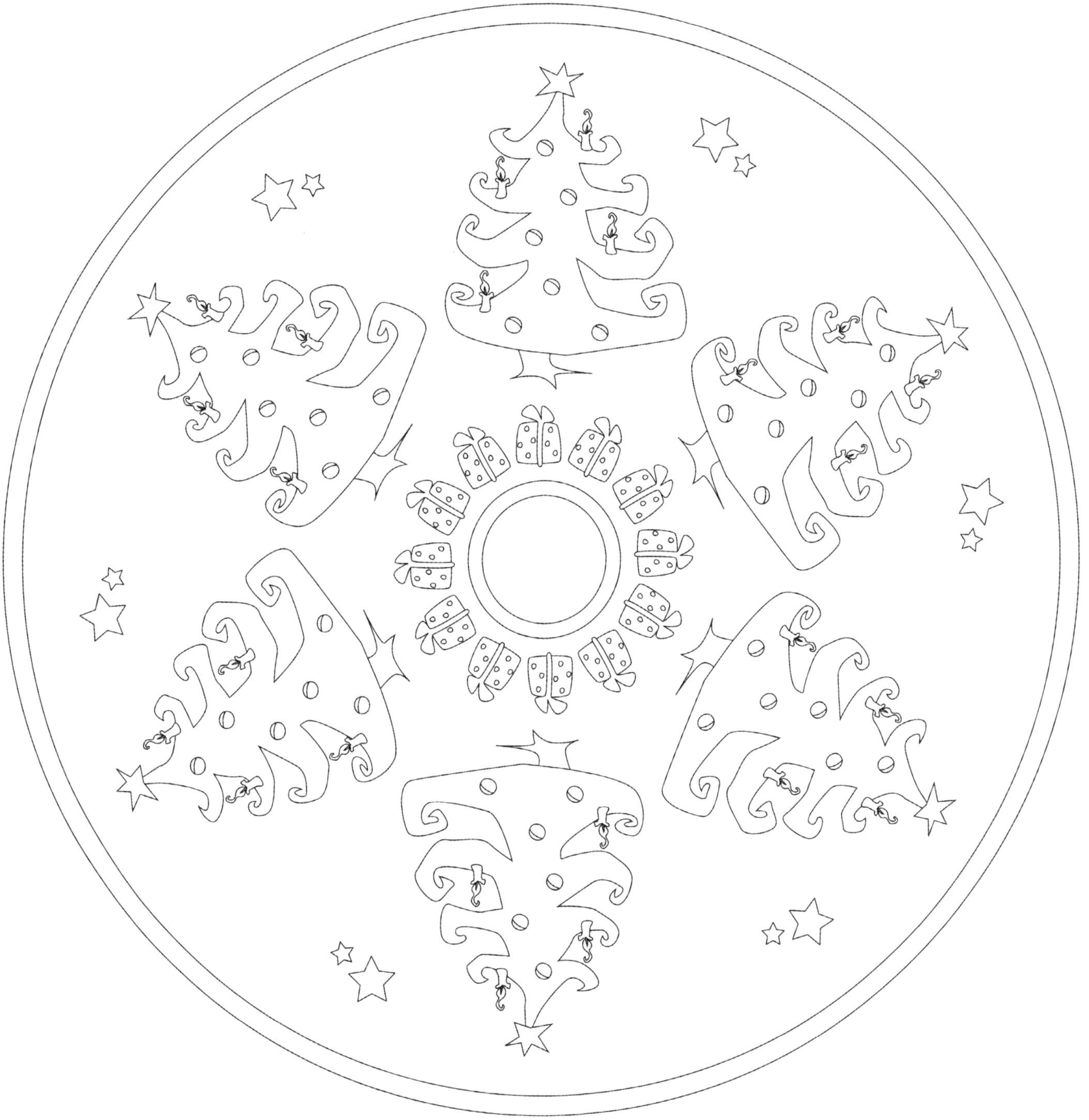

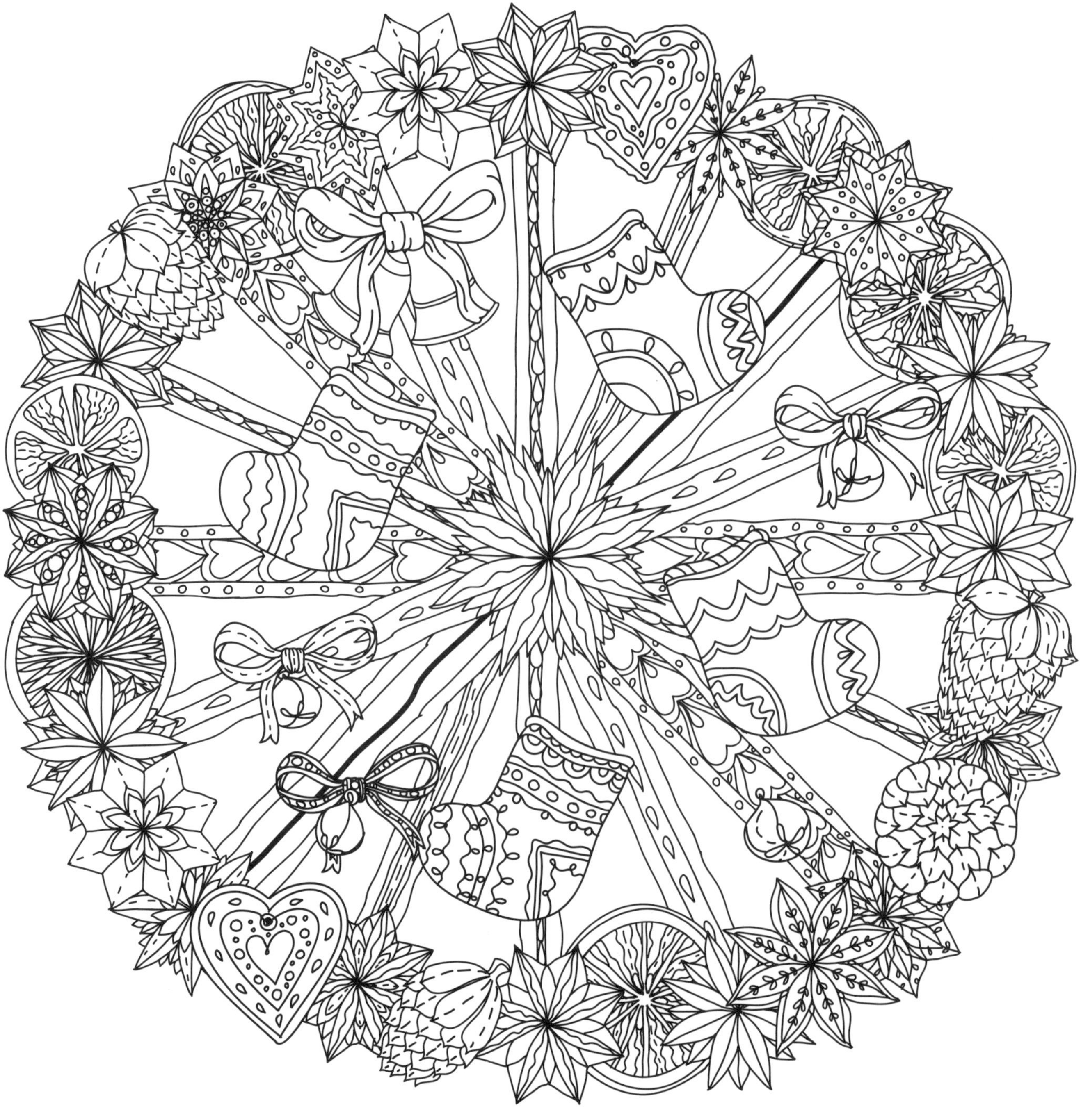

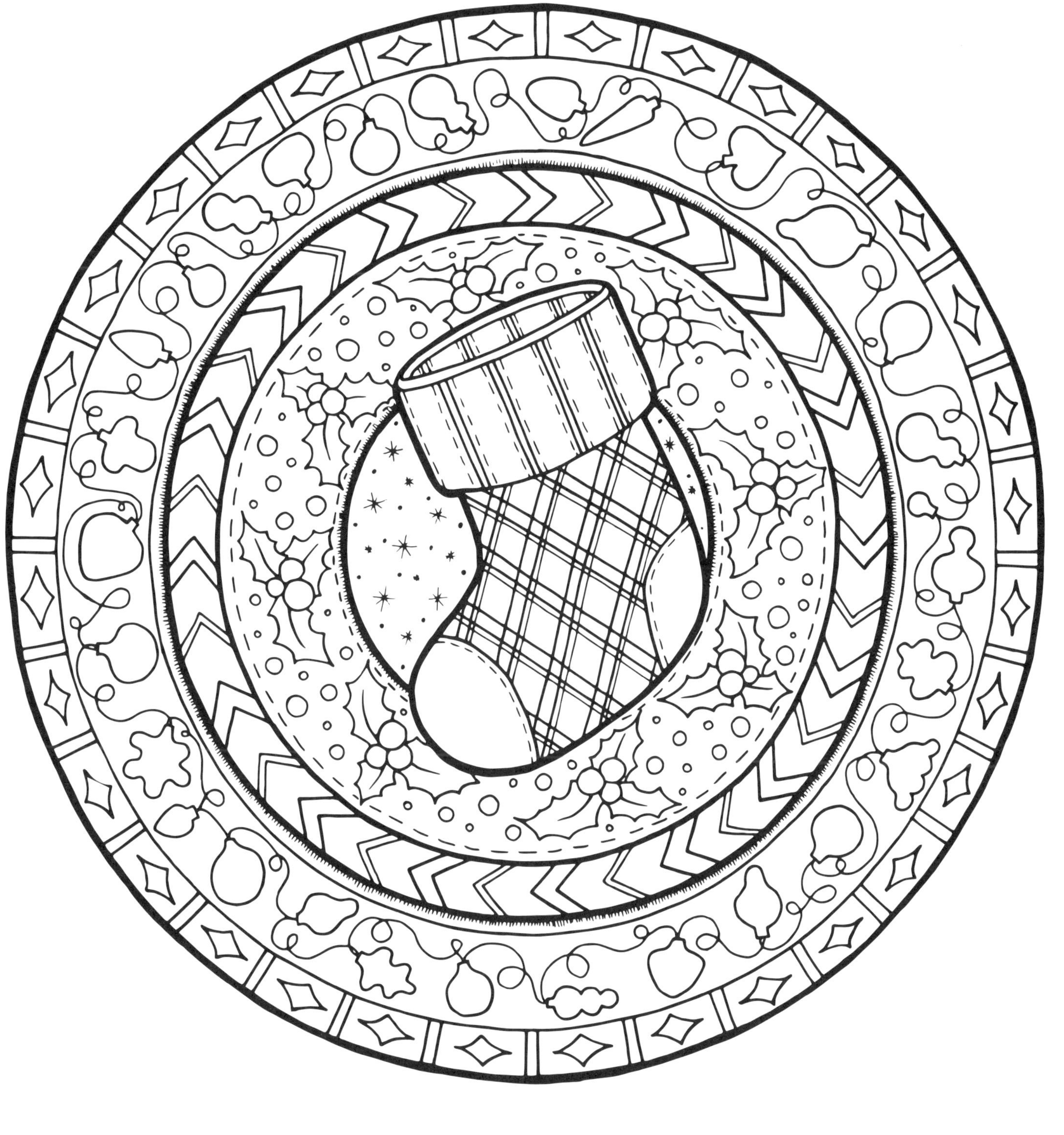

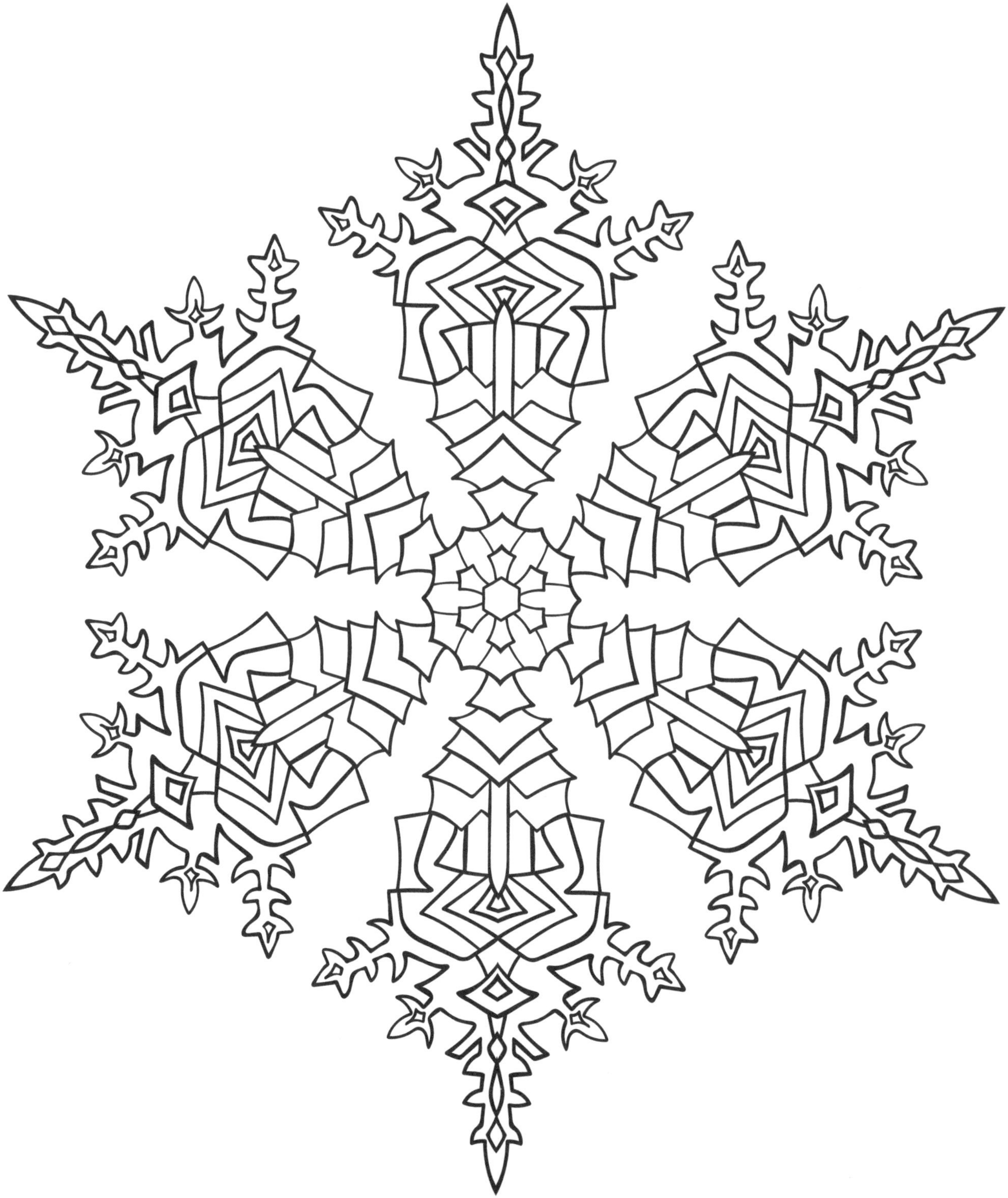

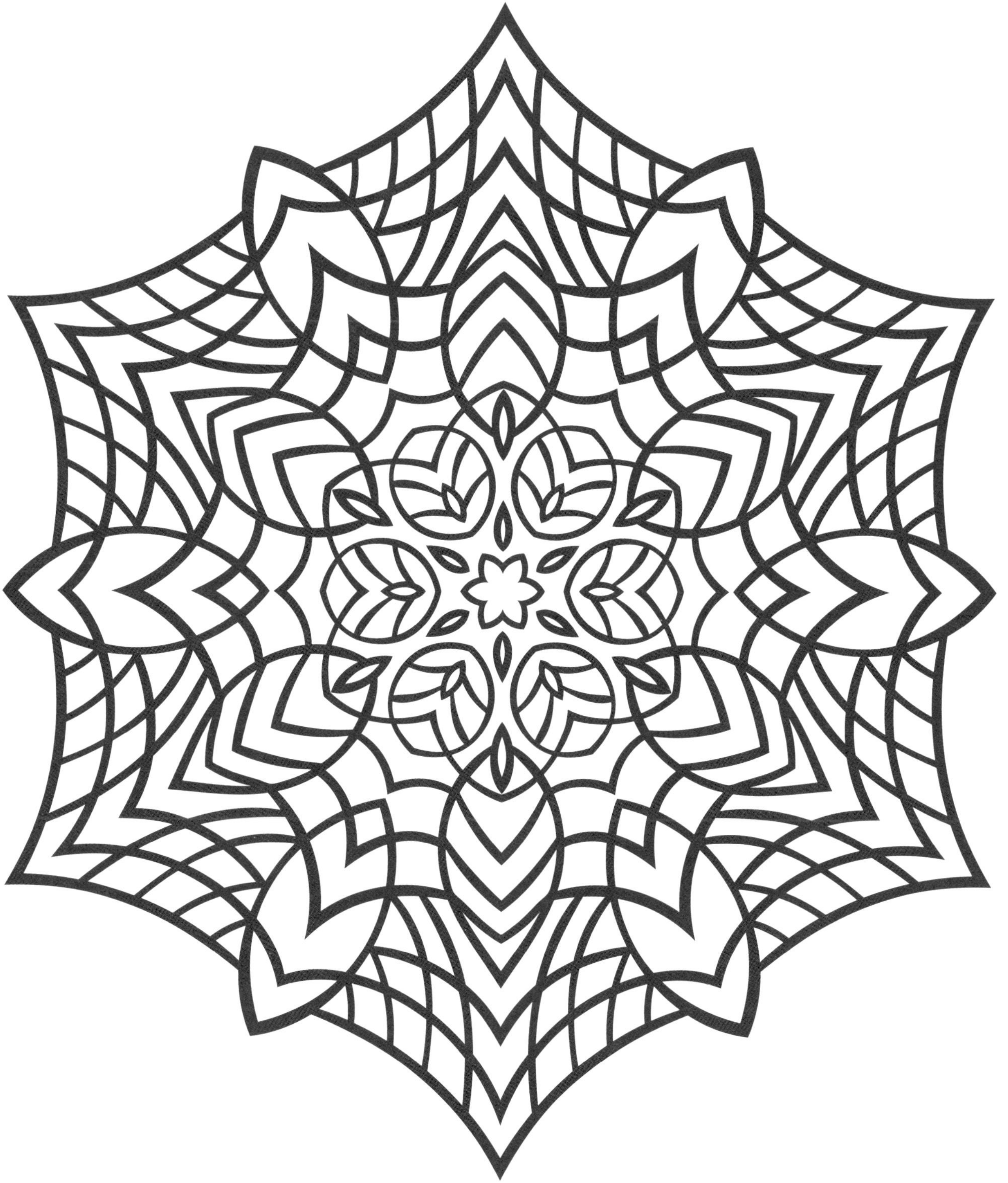

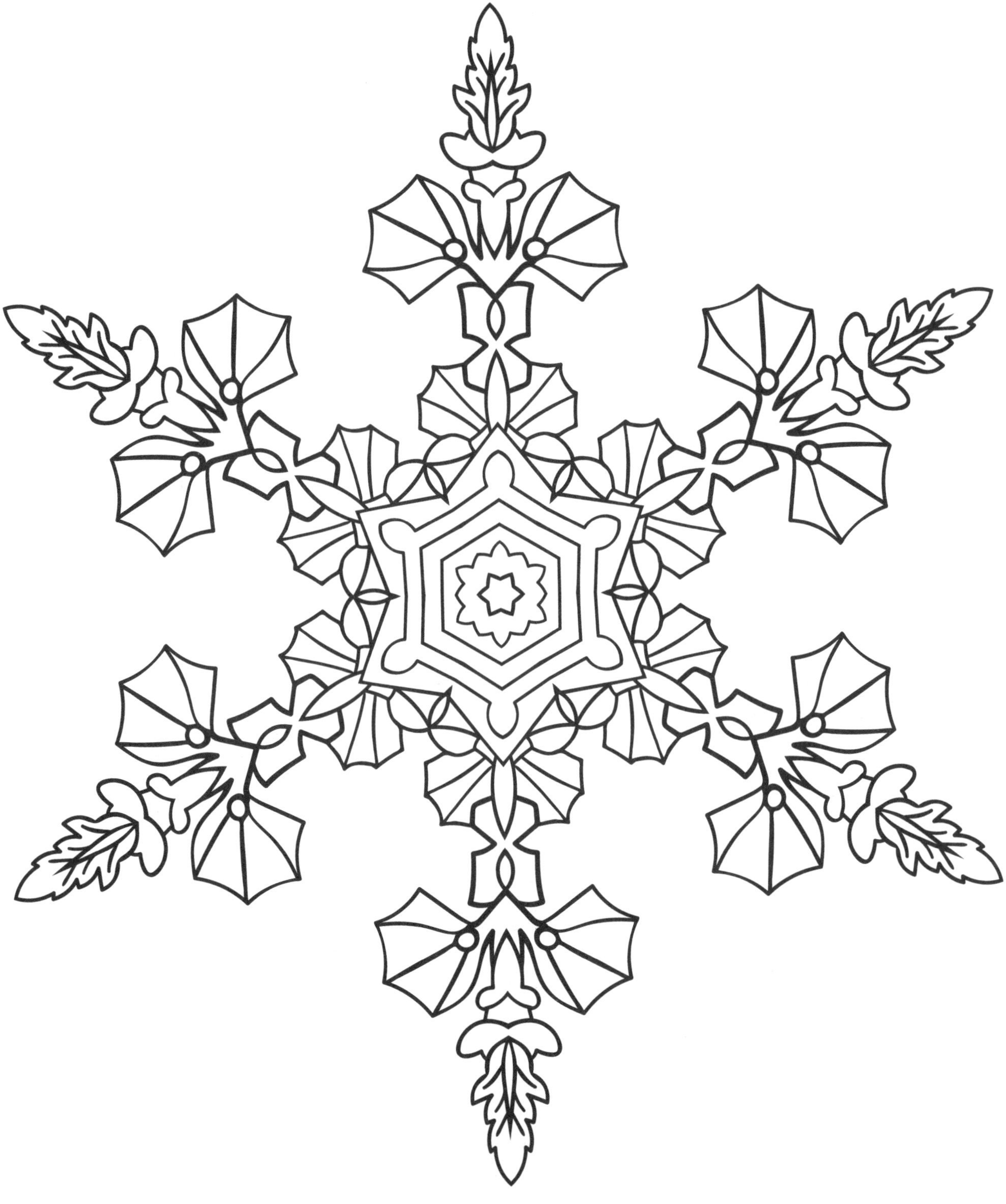

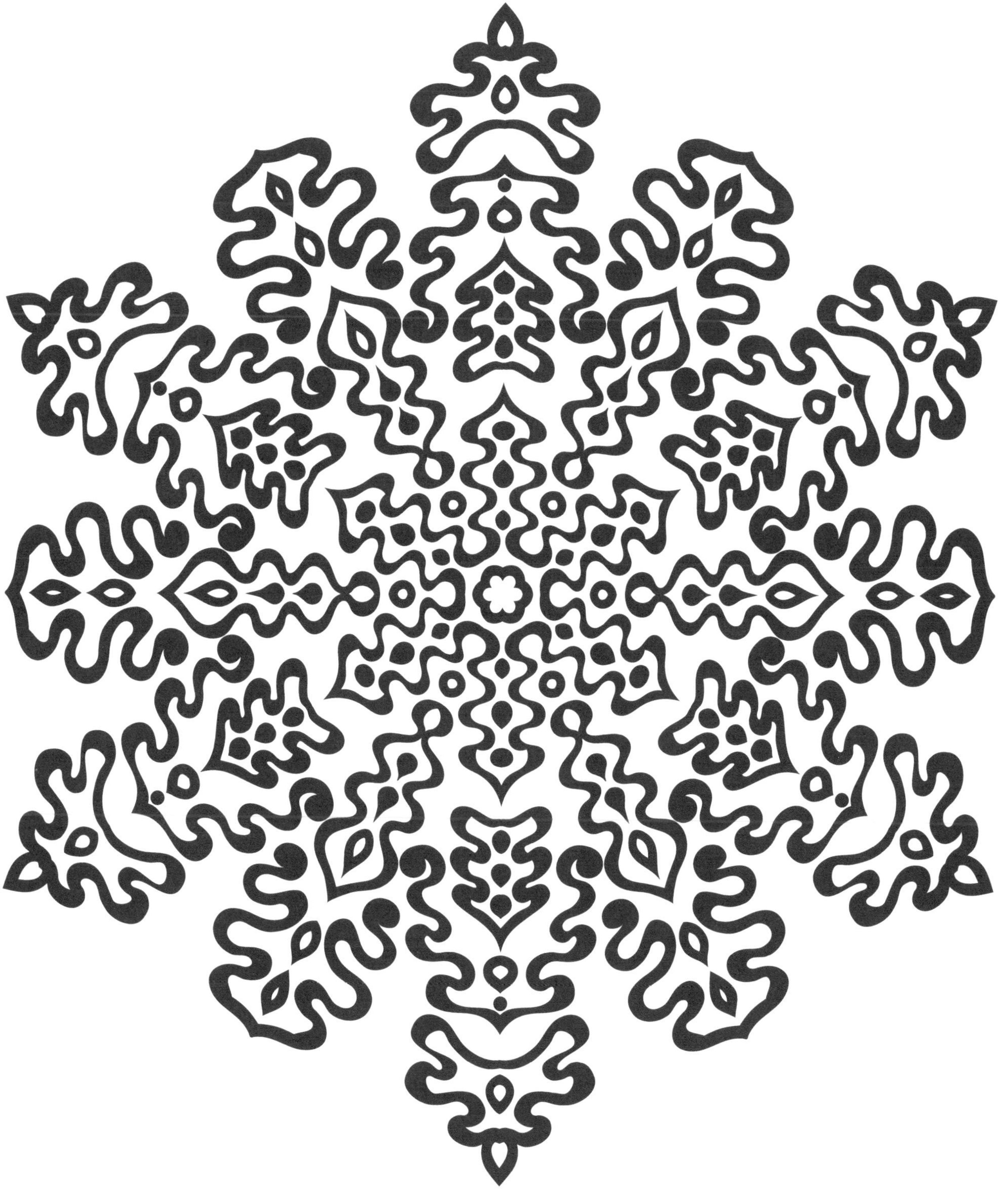

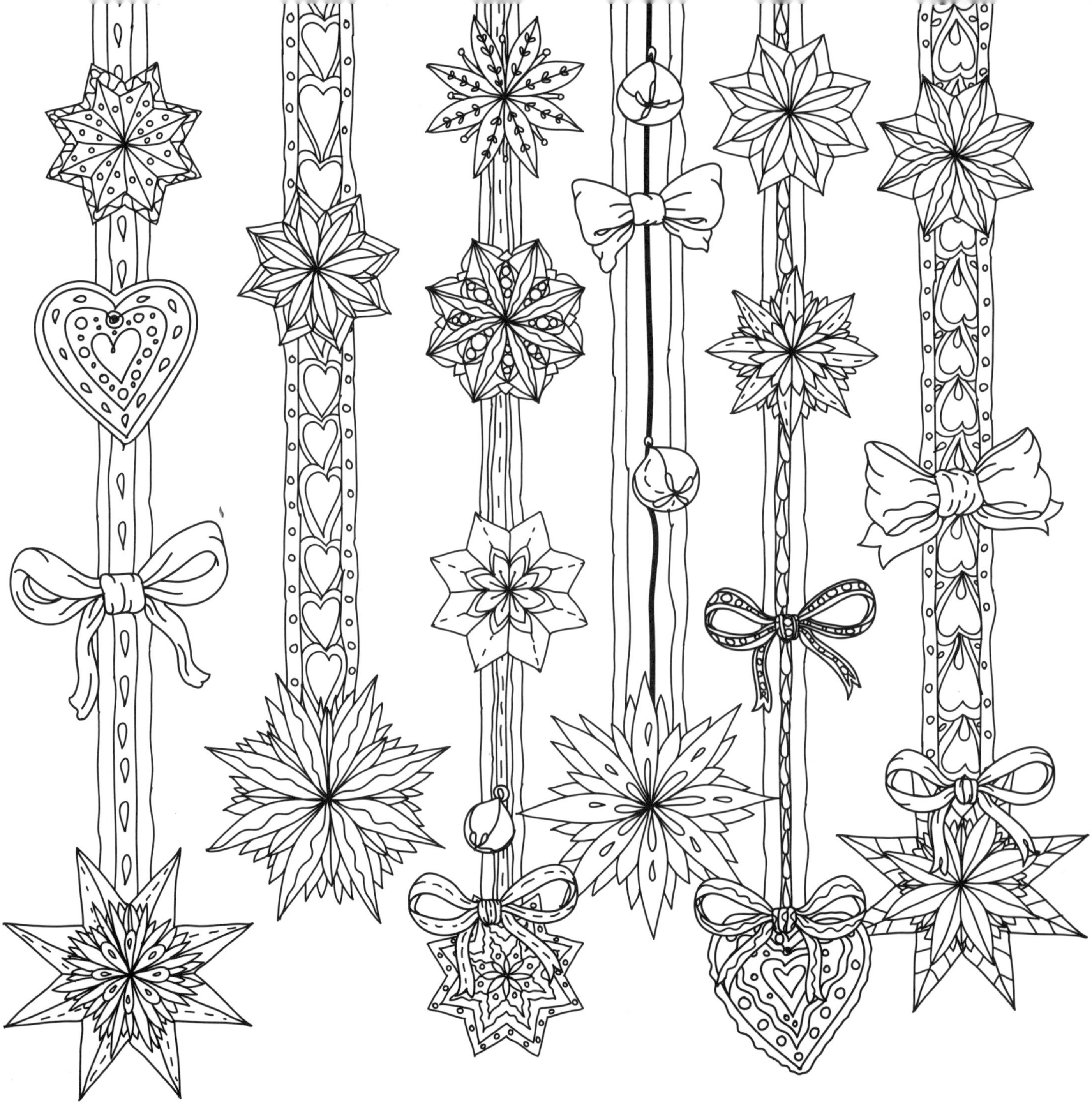

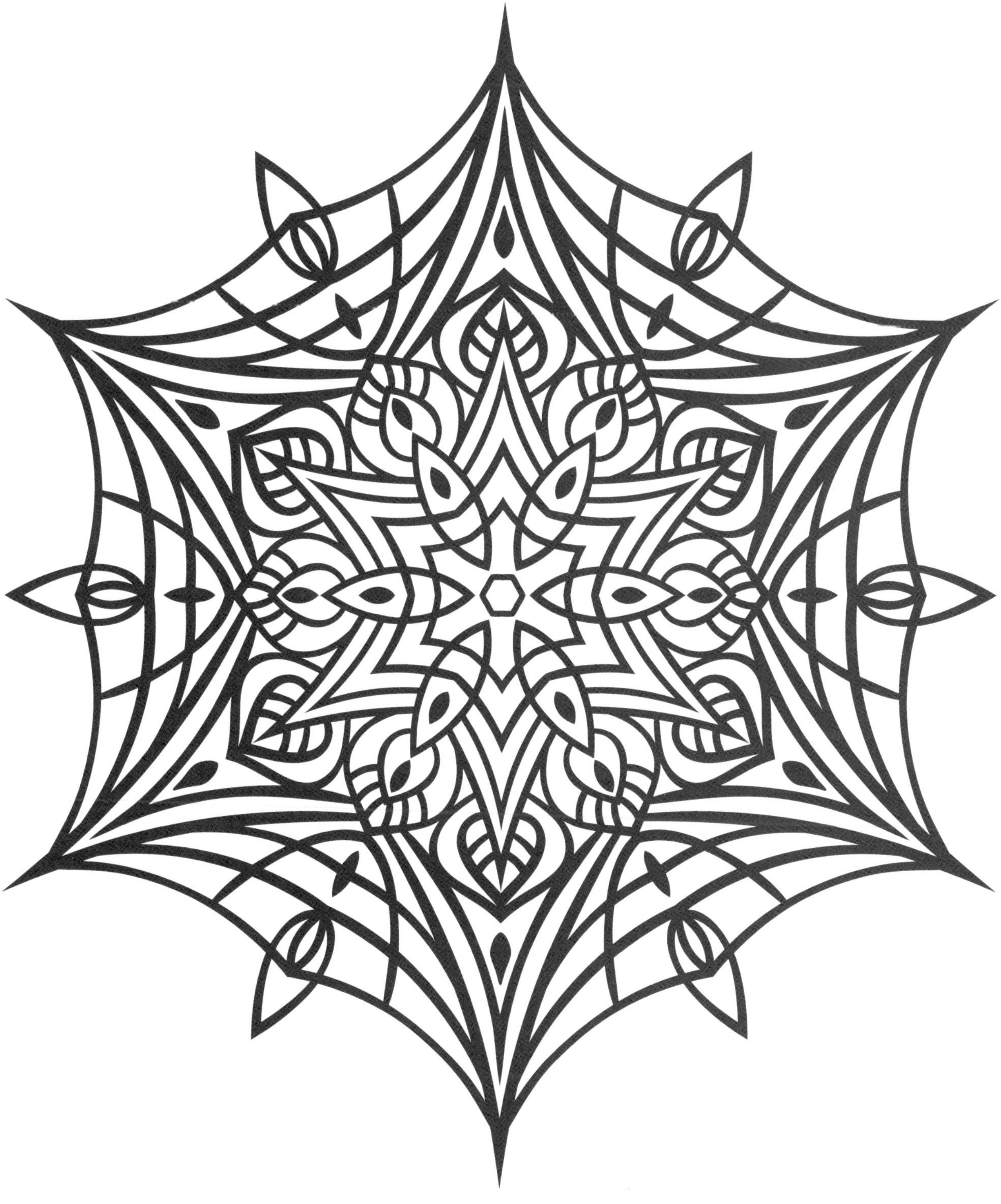

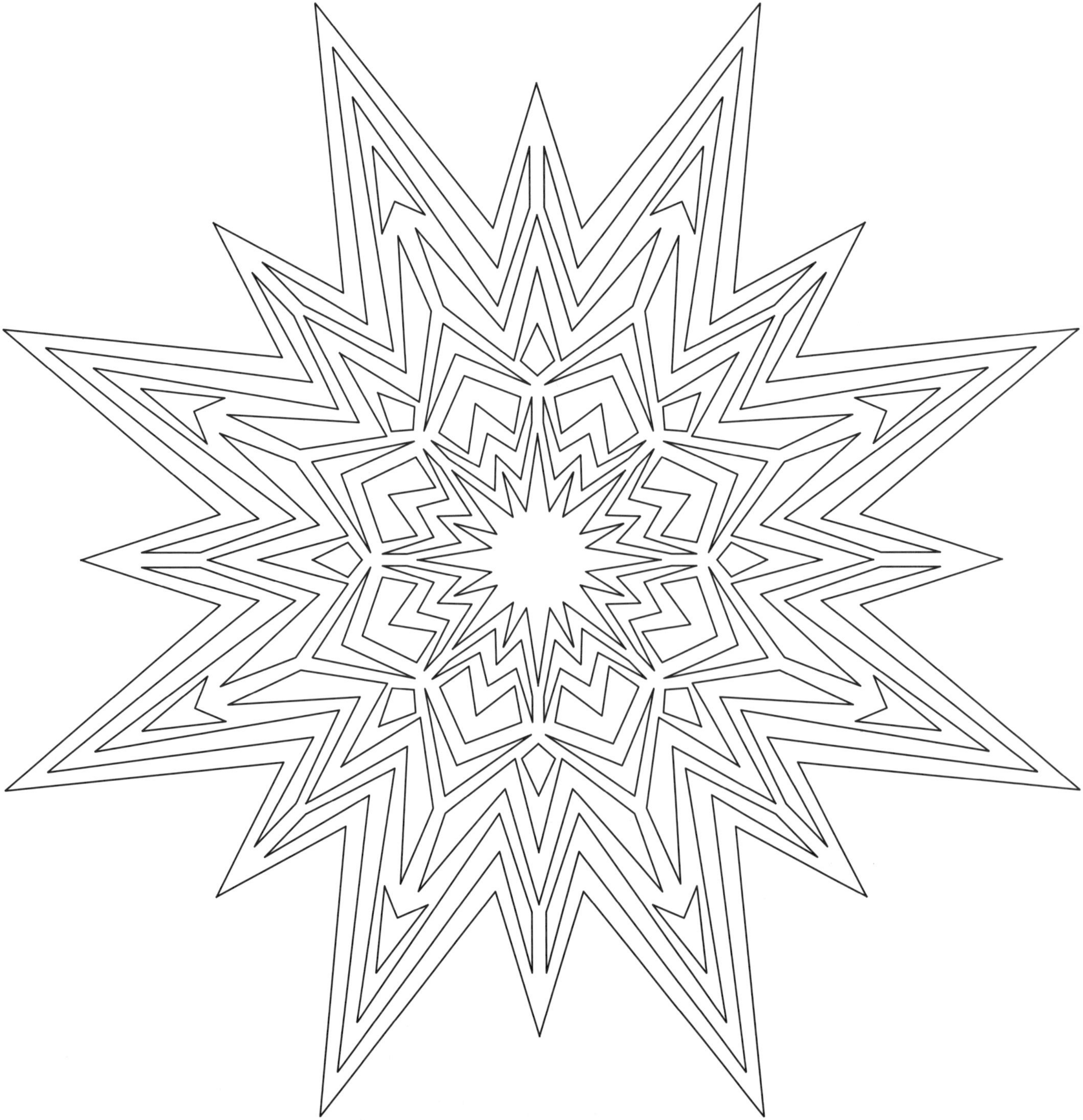

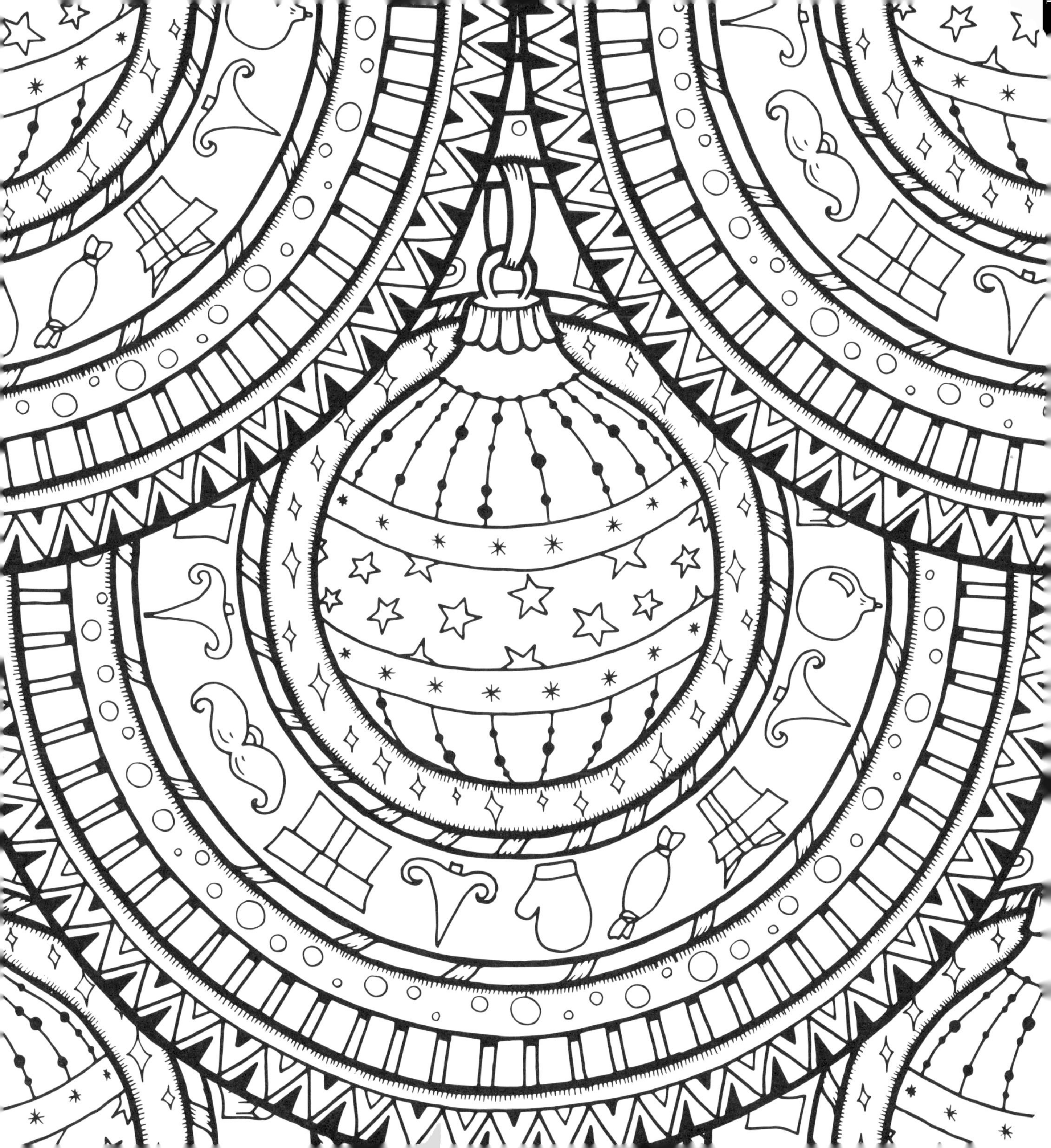

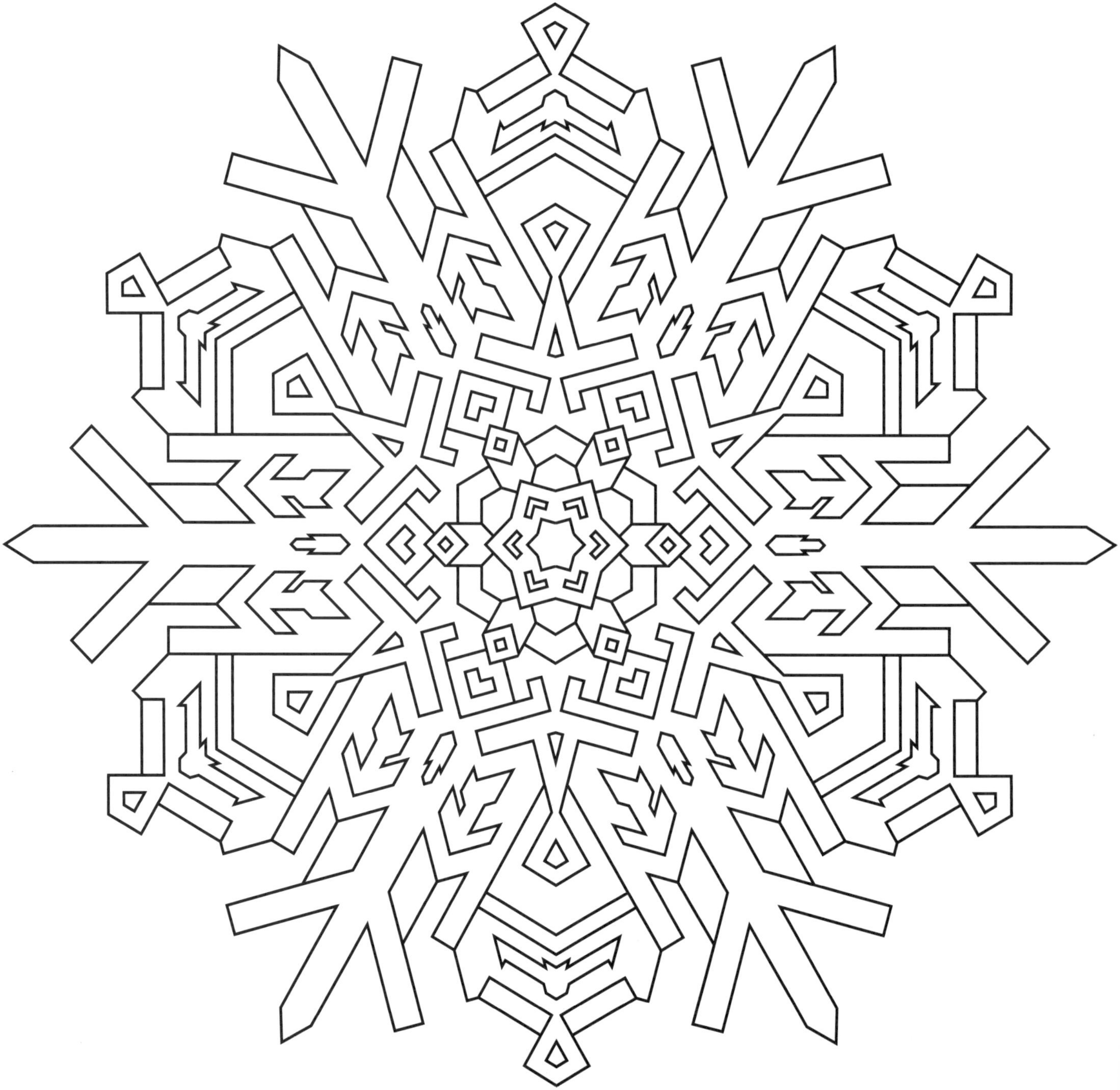

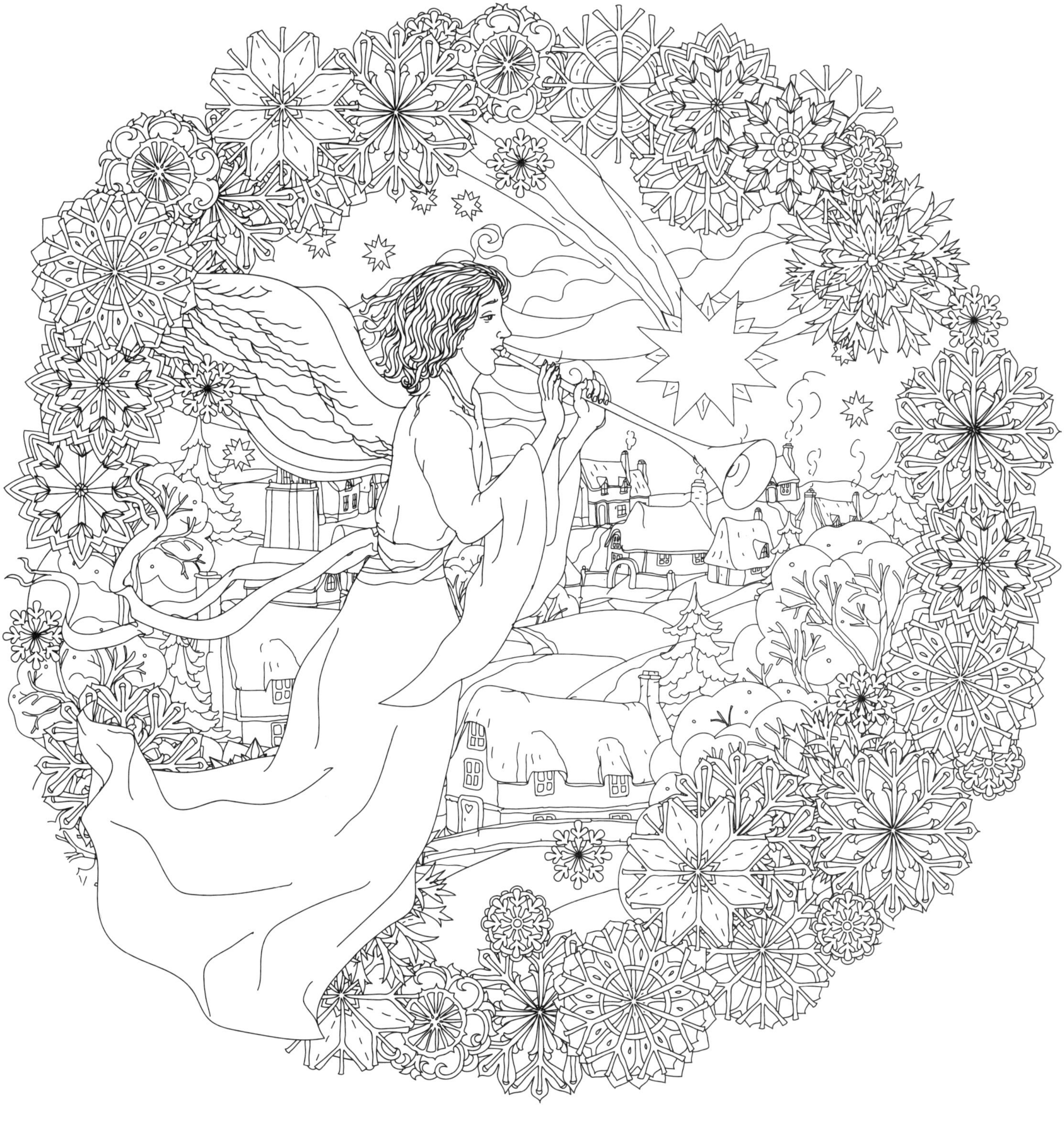

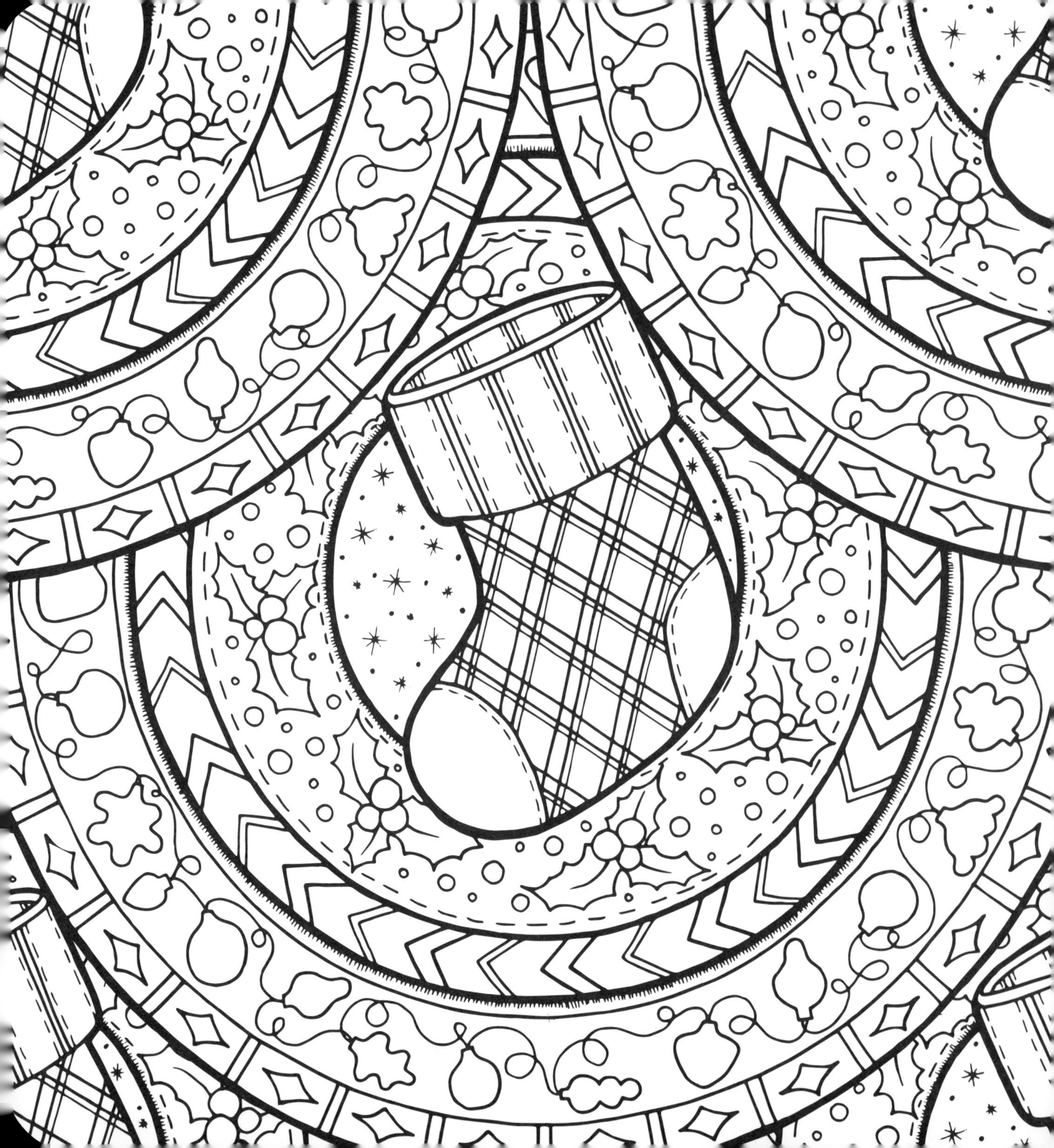

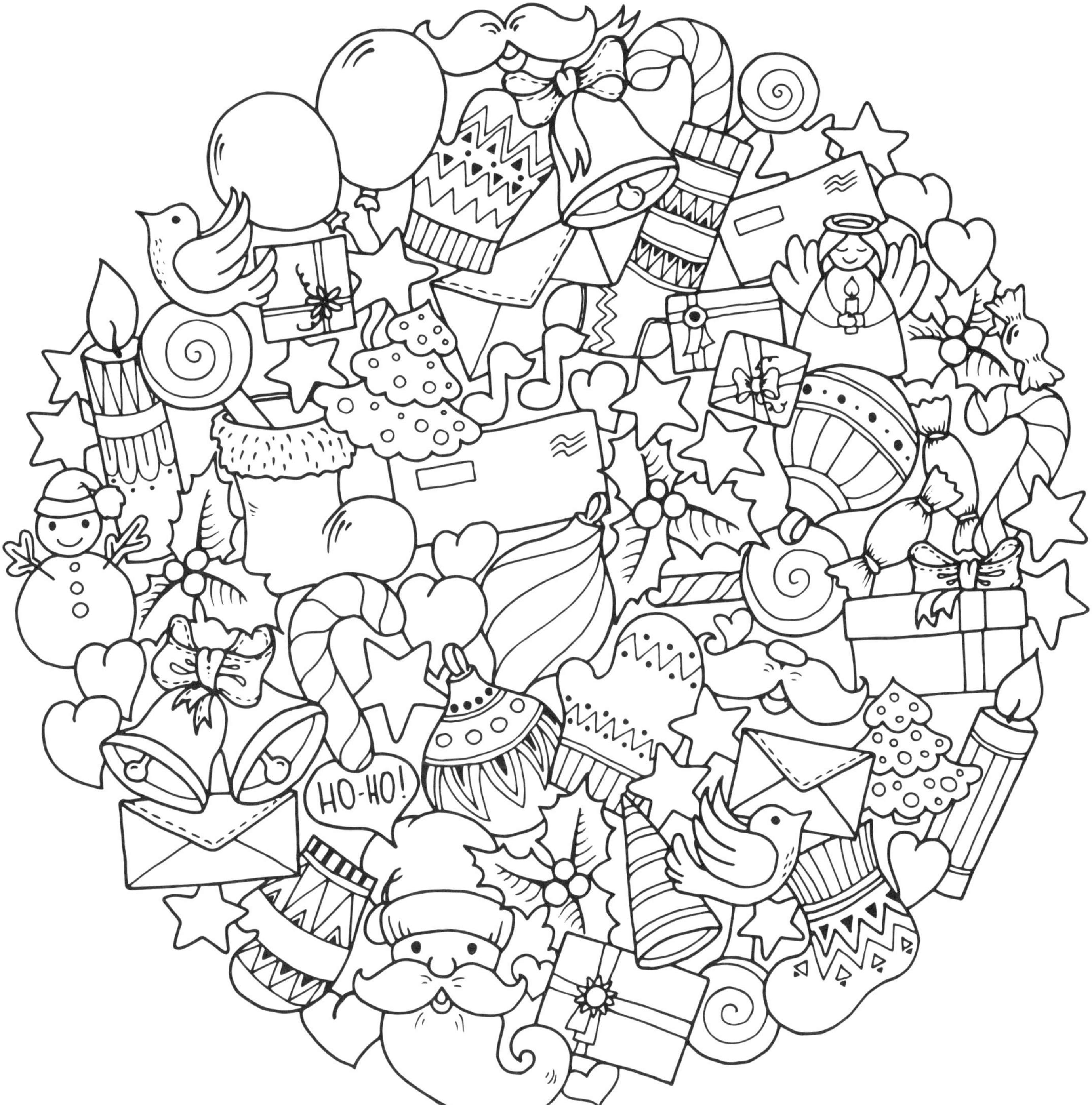
HO-HO!

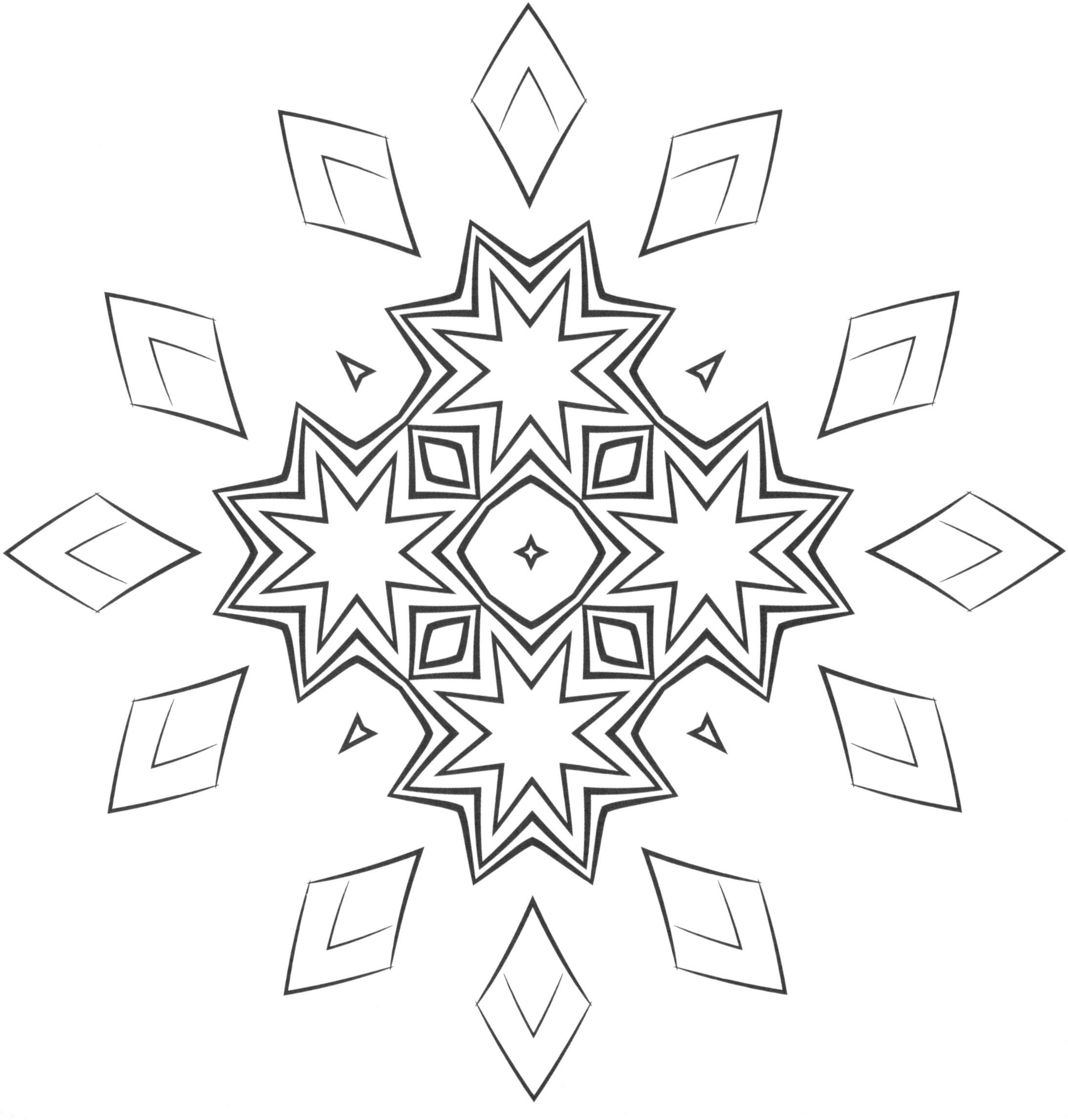

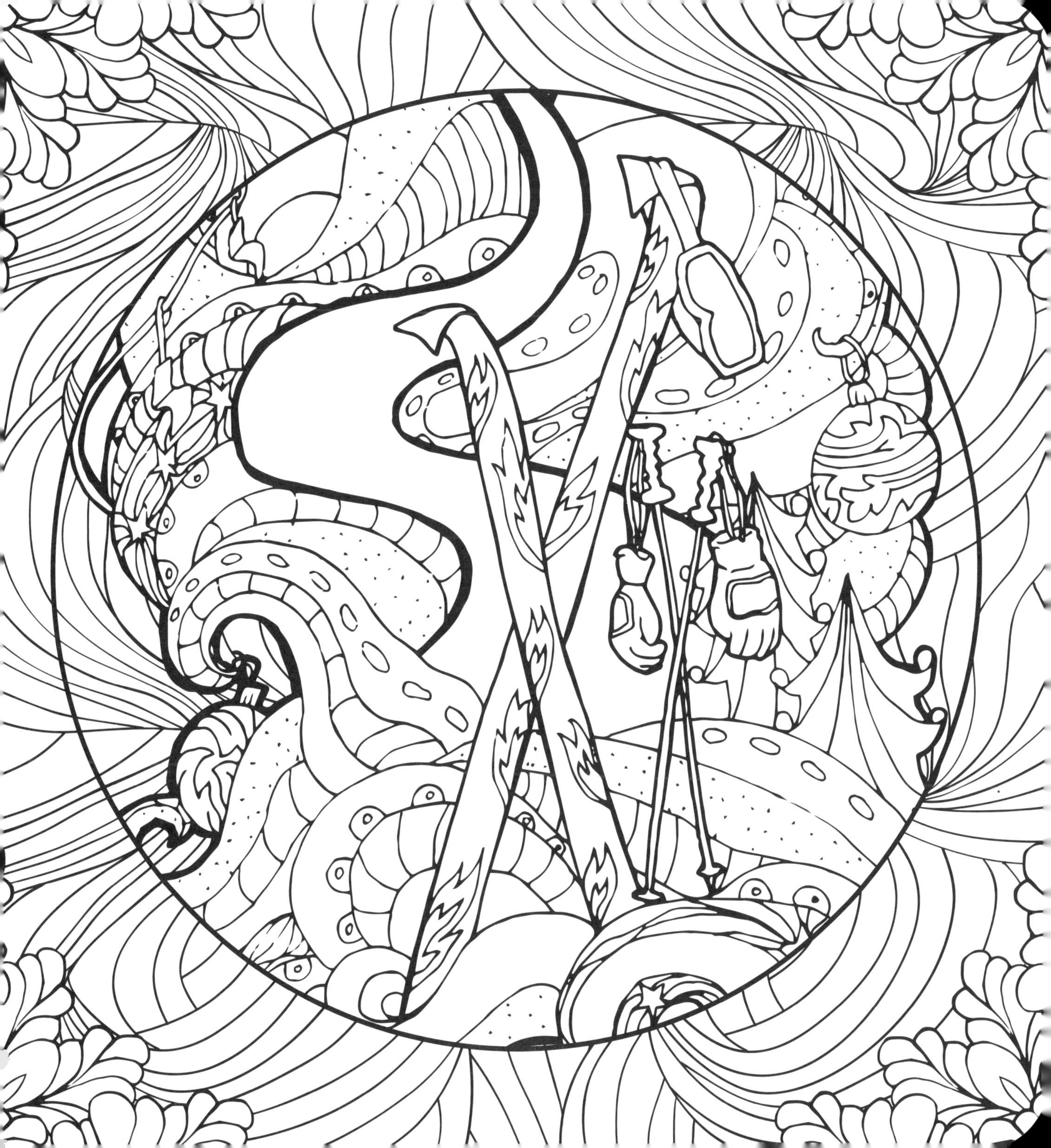

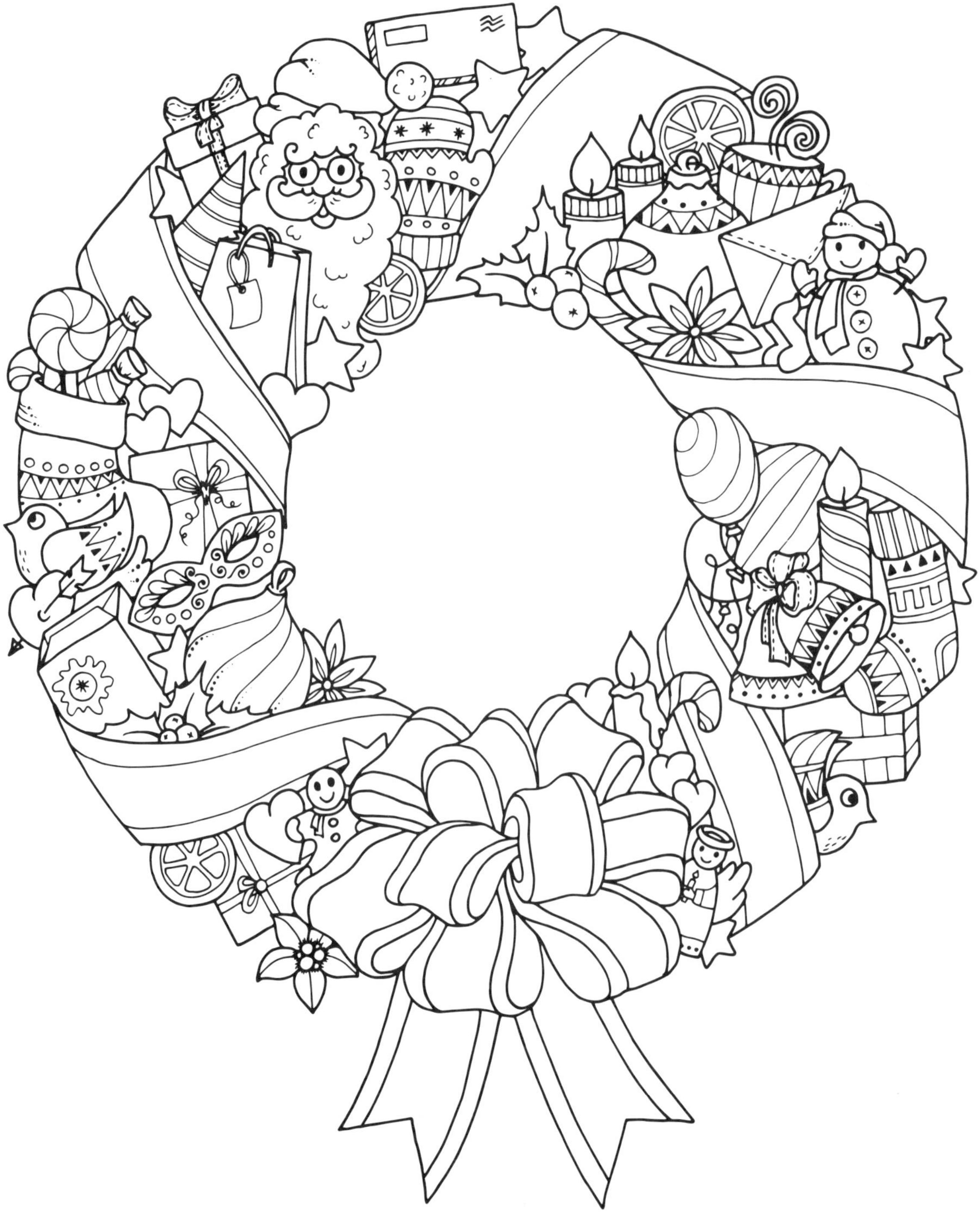

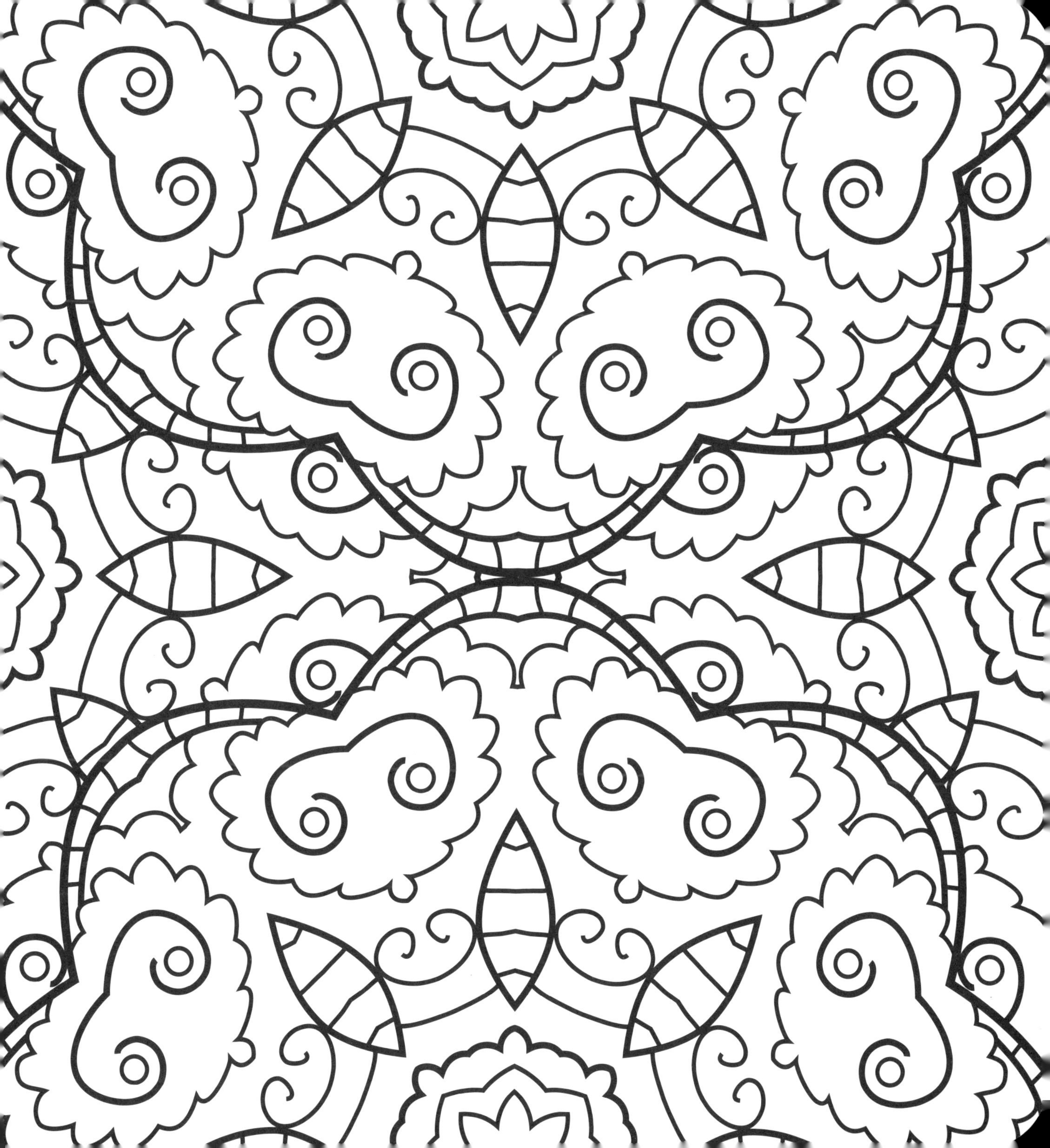

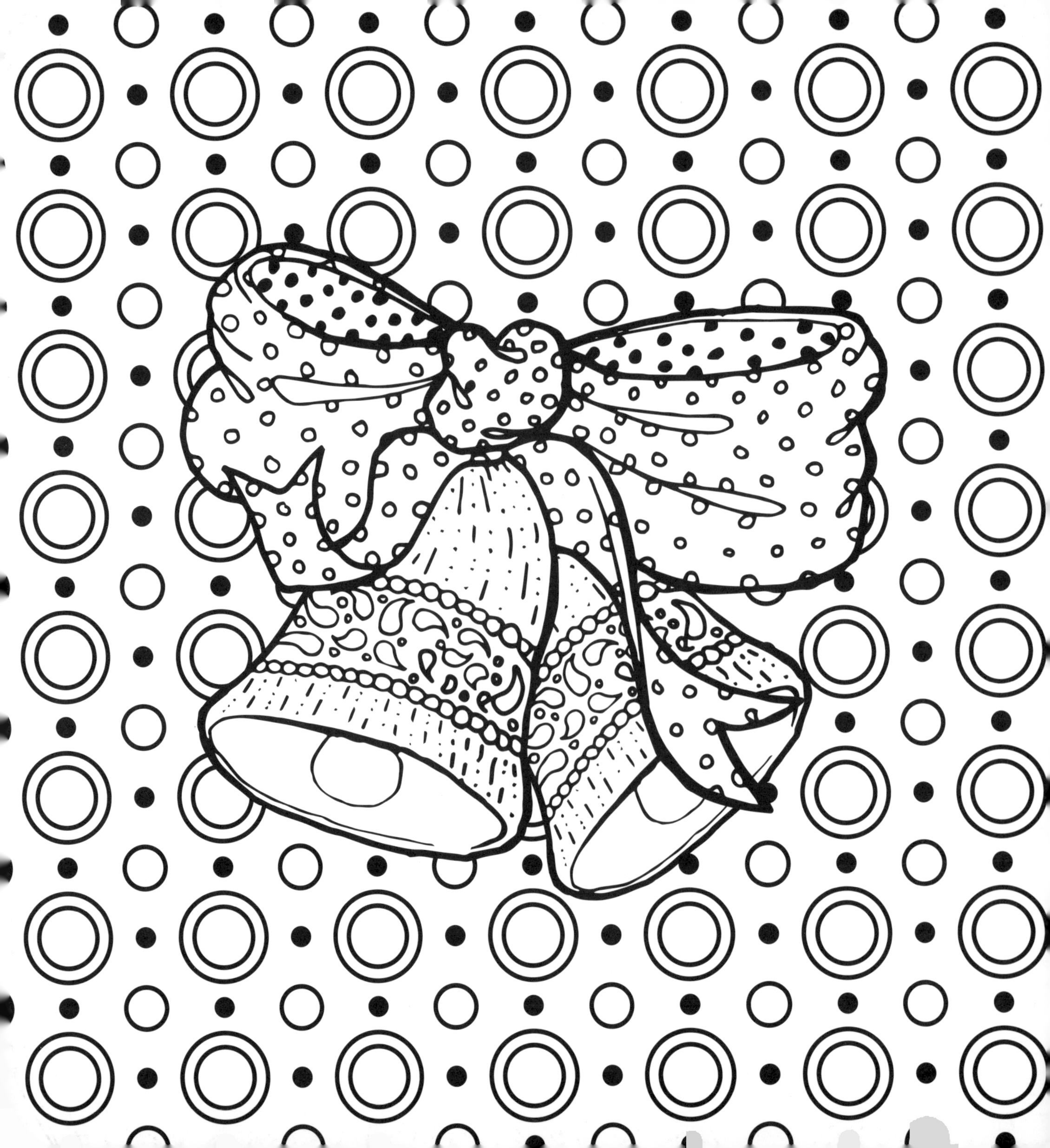

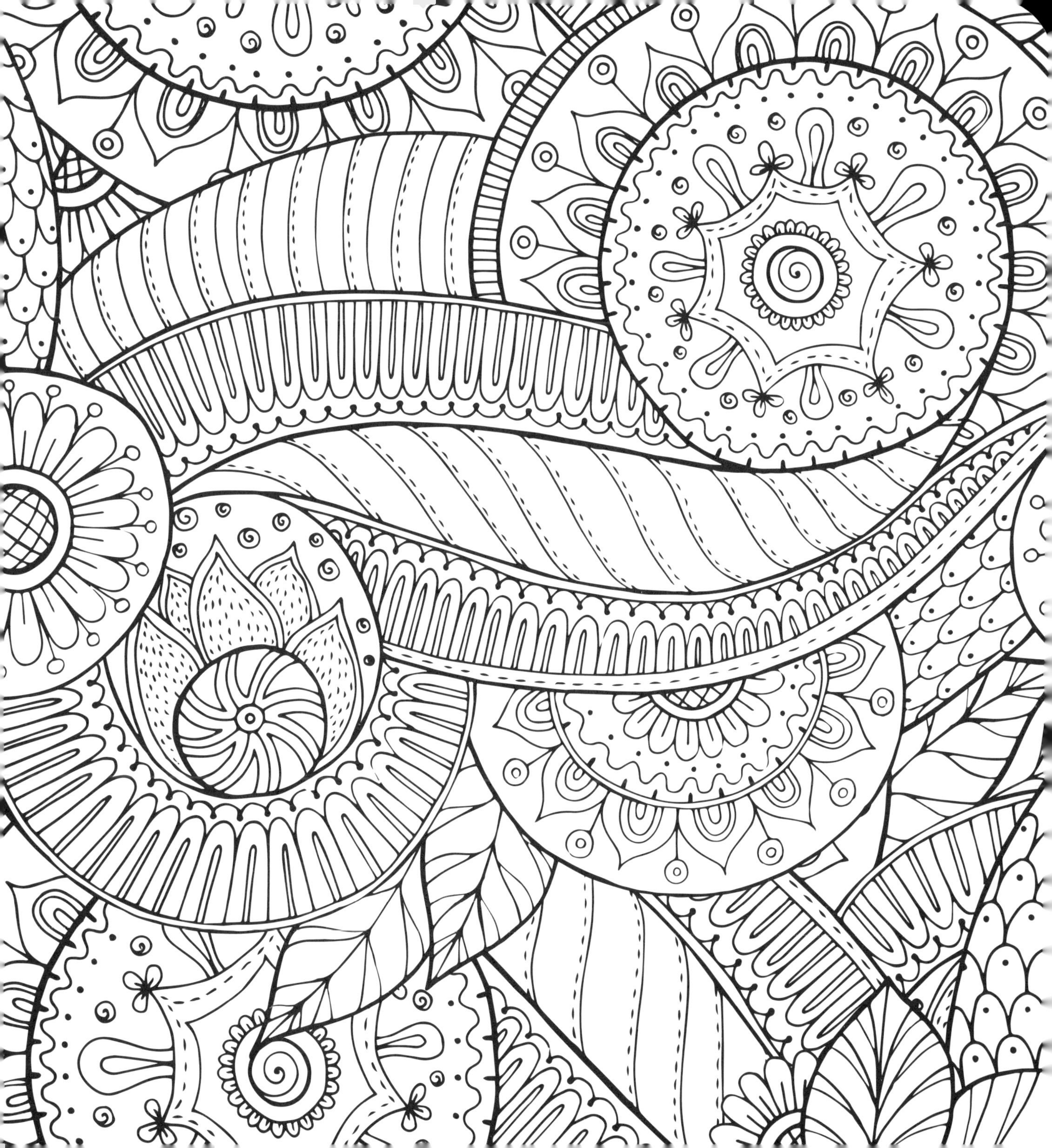

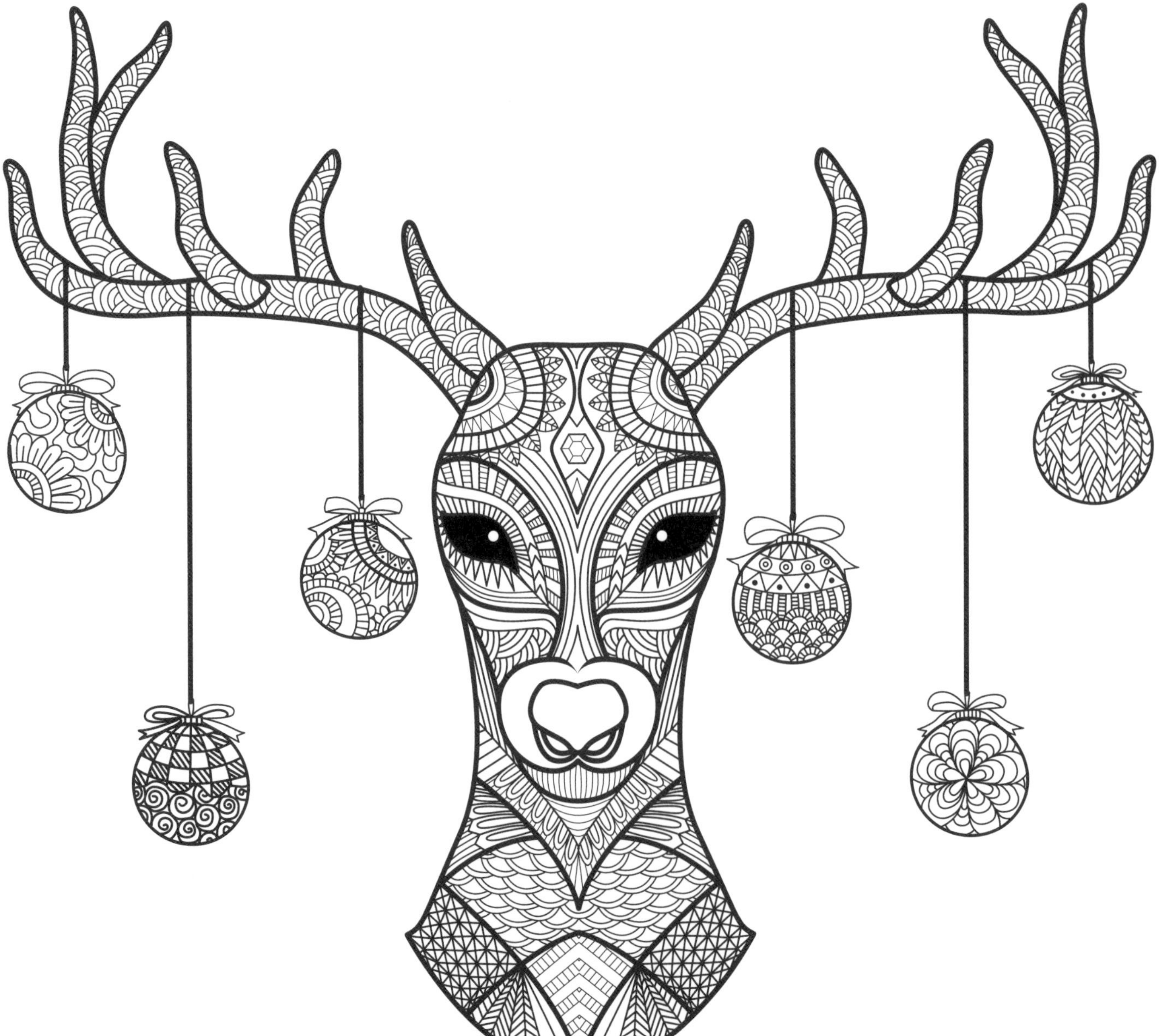

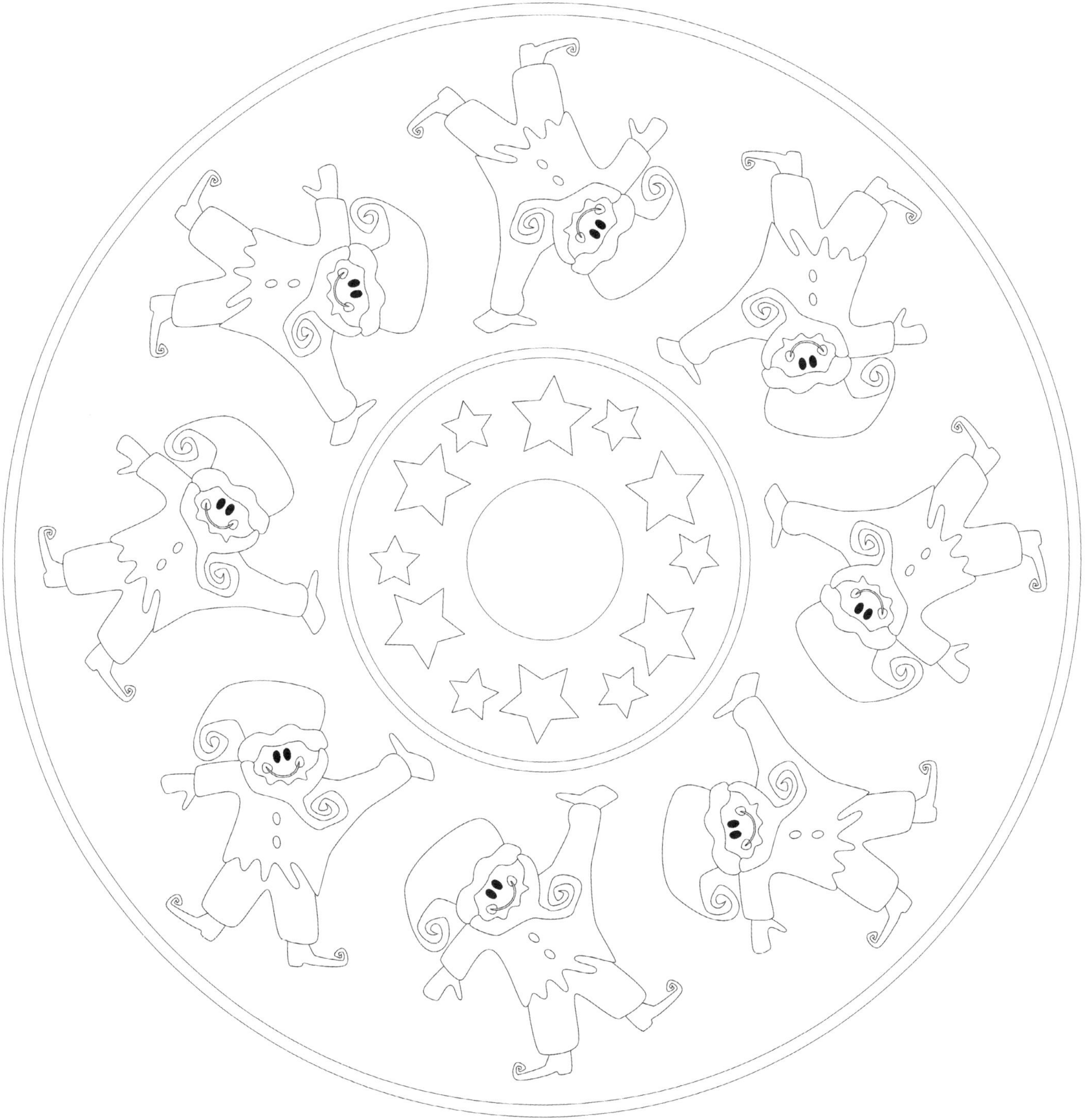

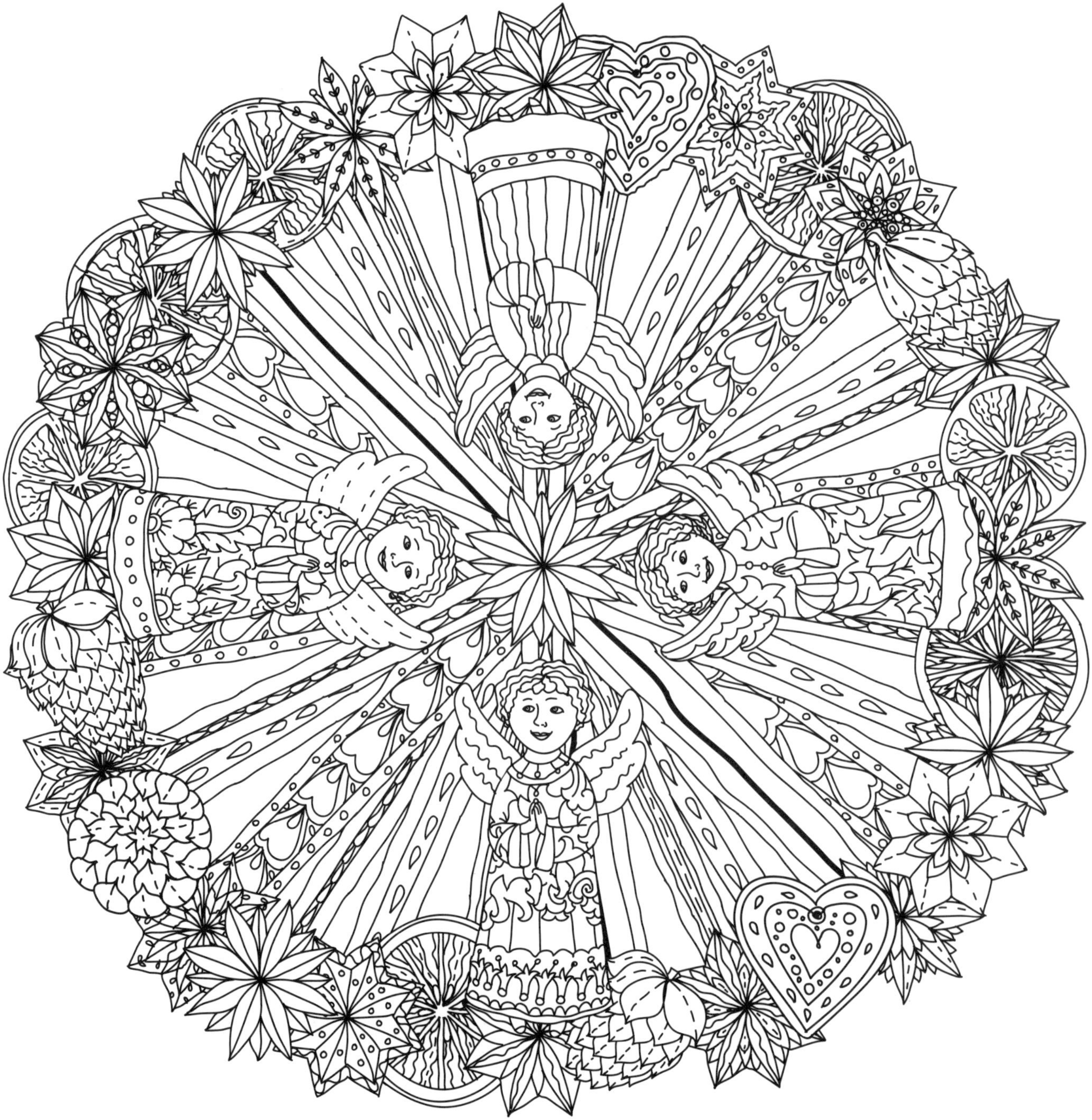

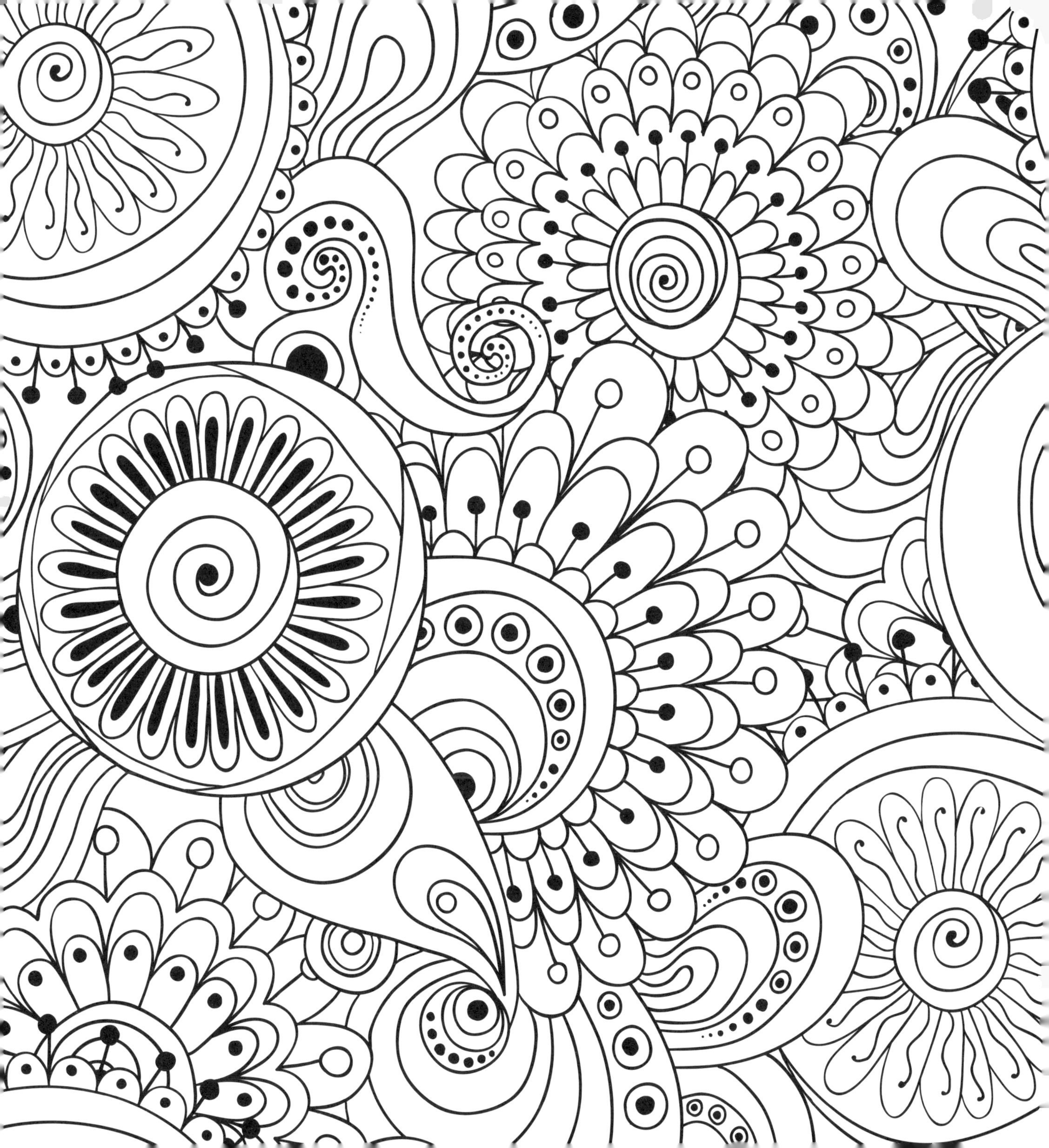

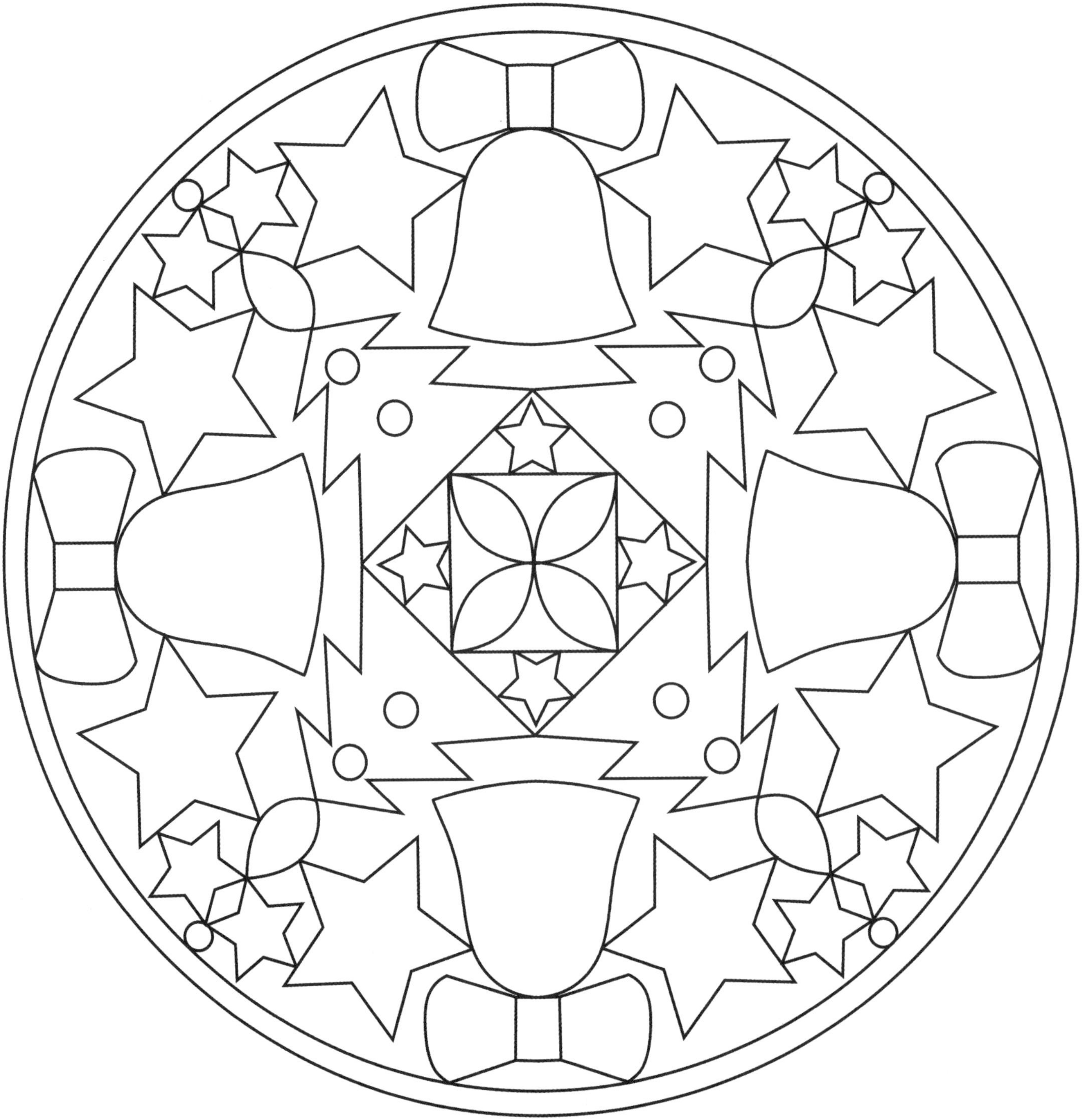

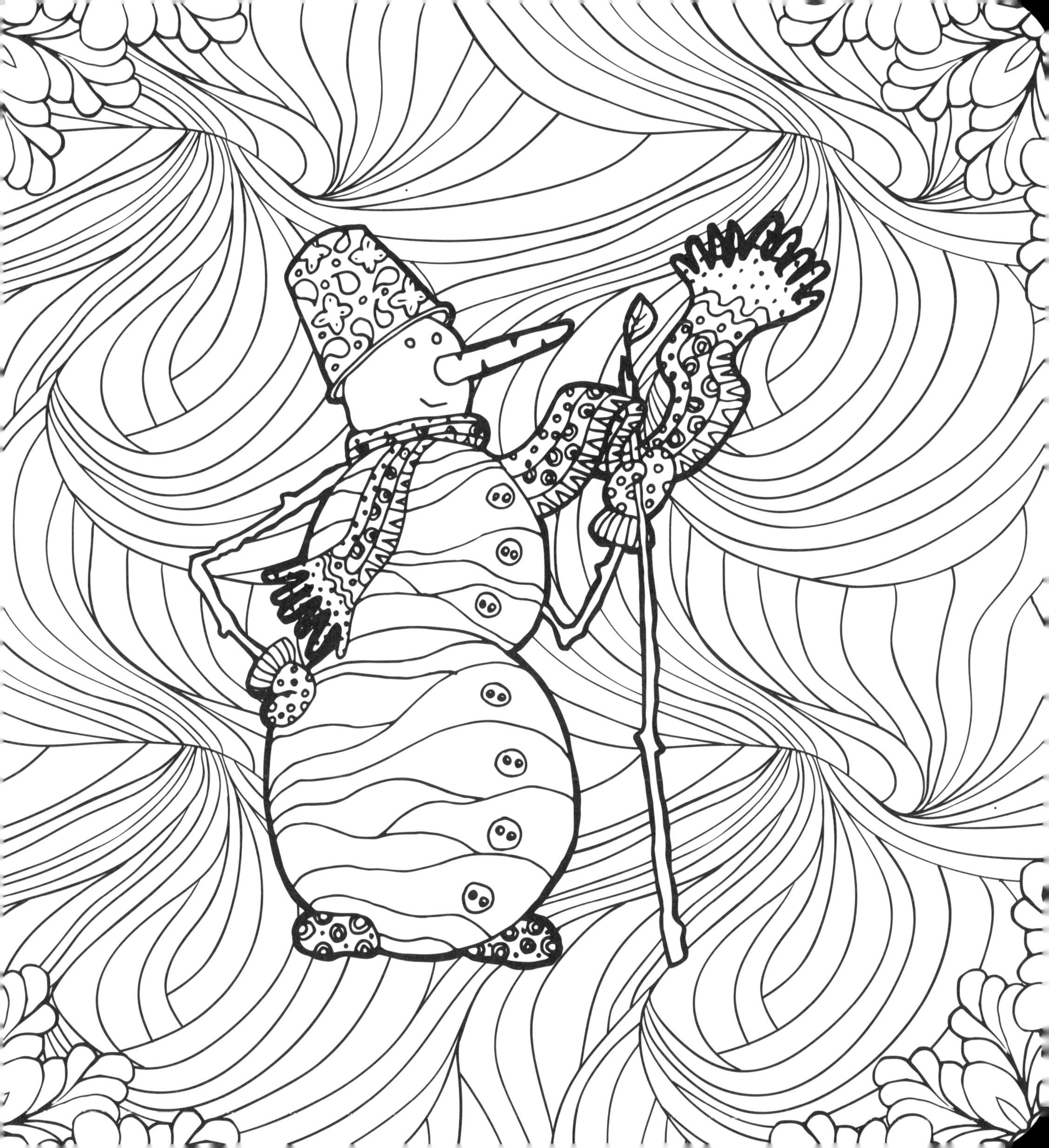

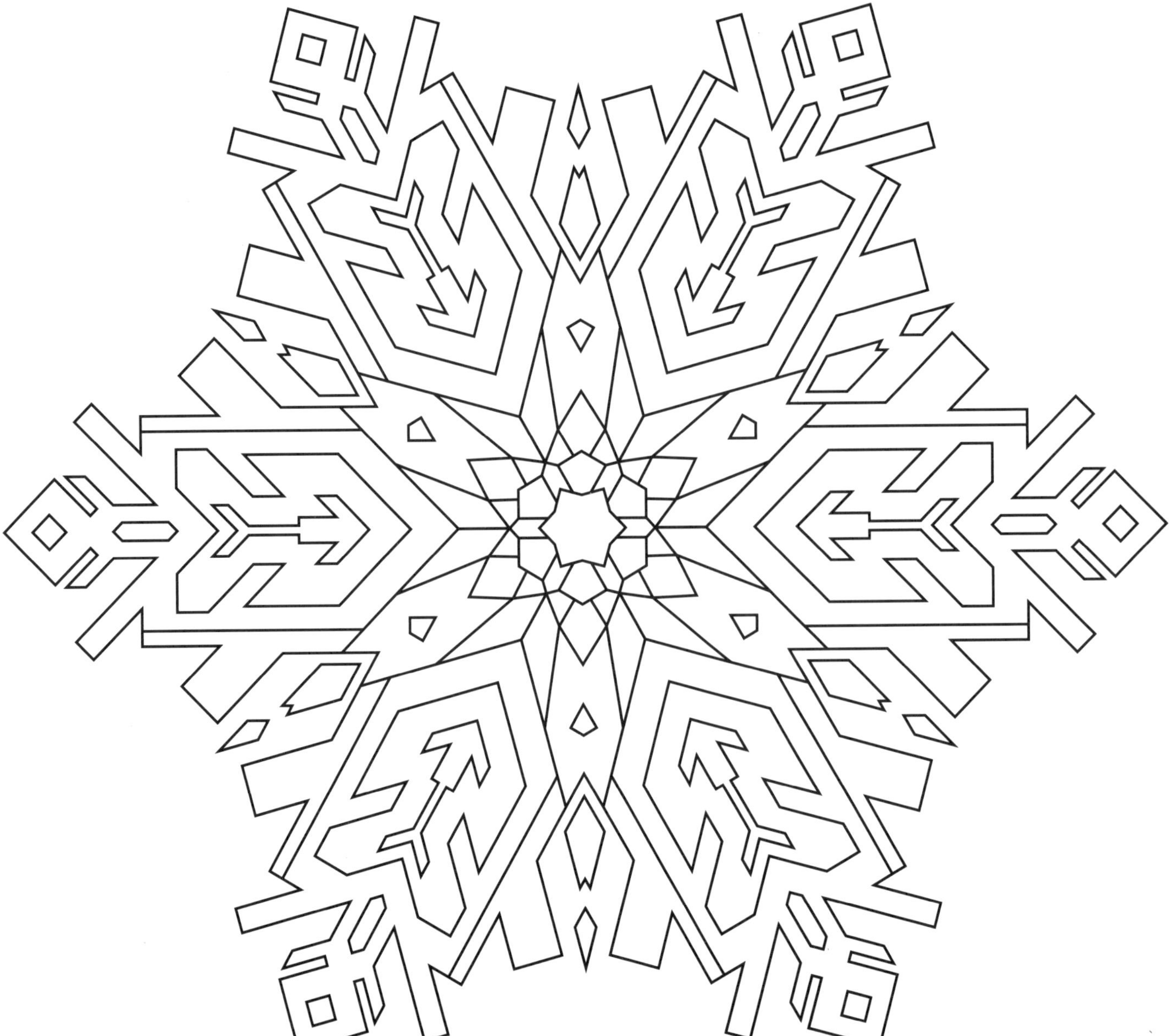

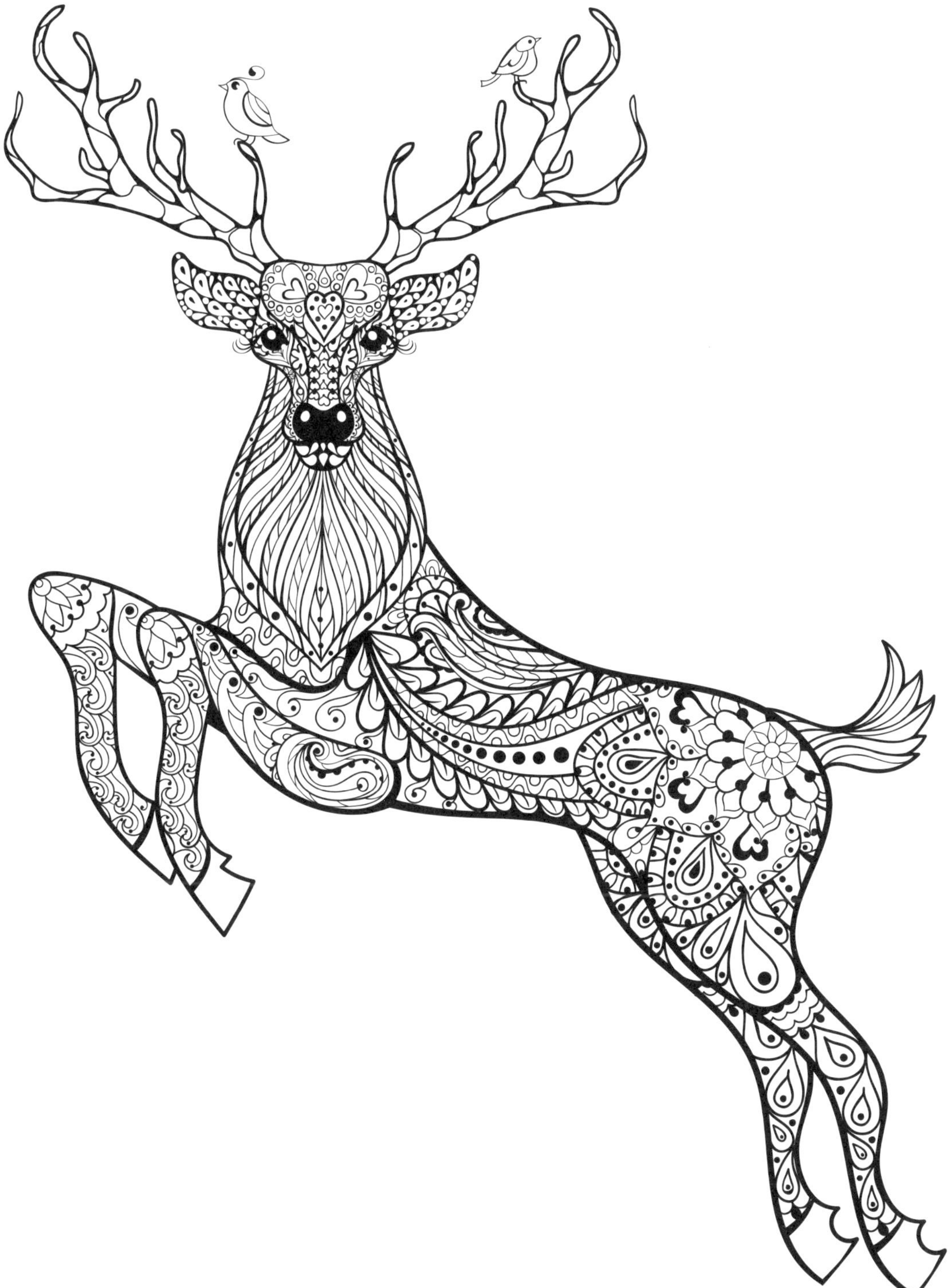

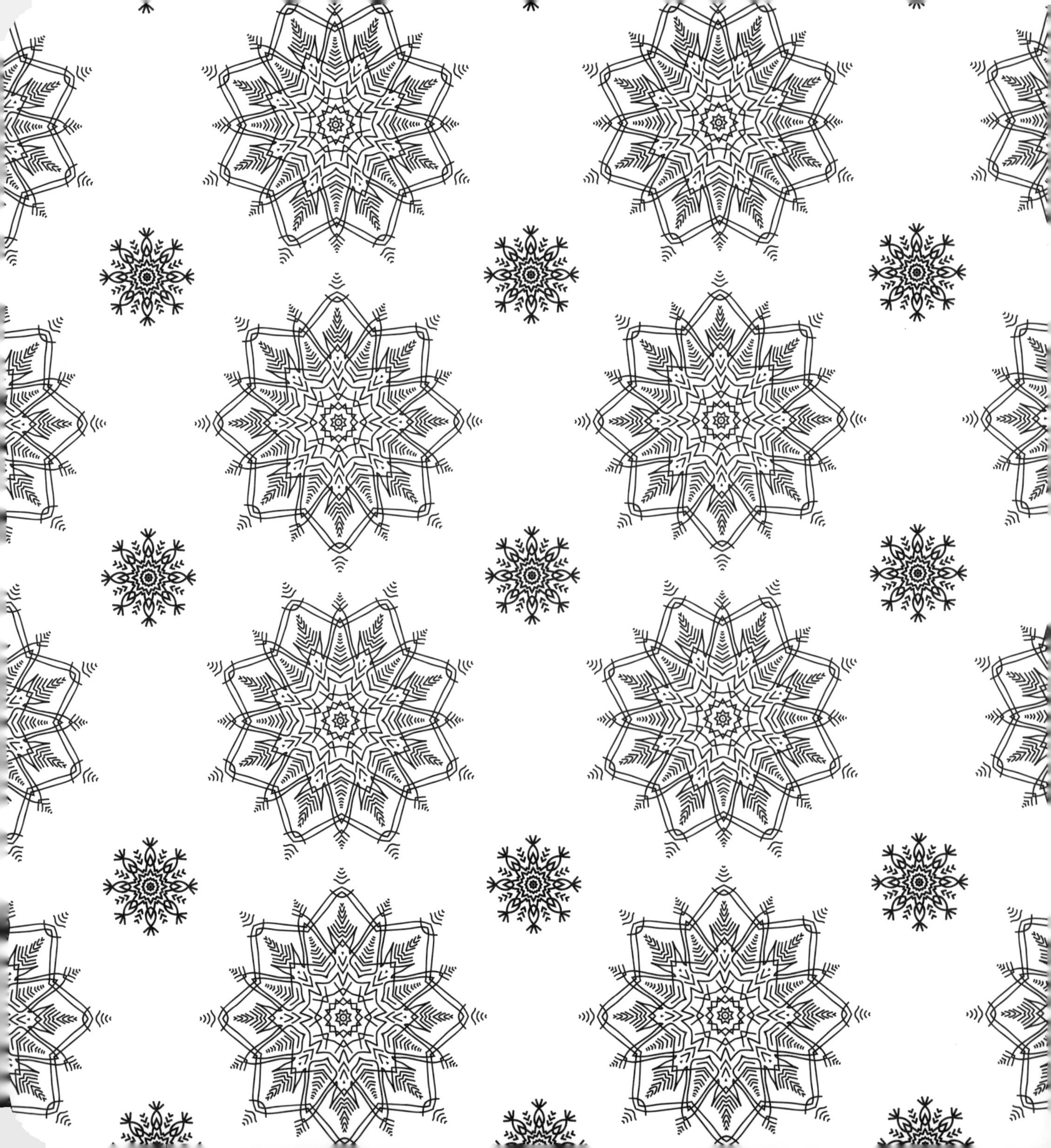

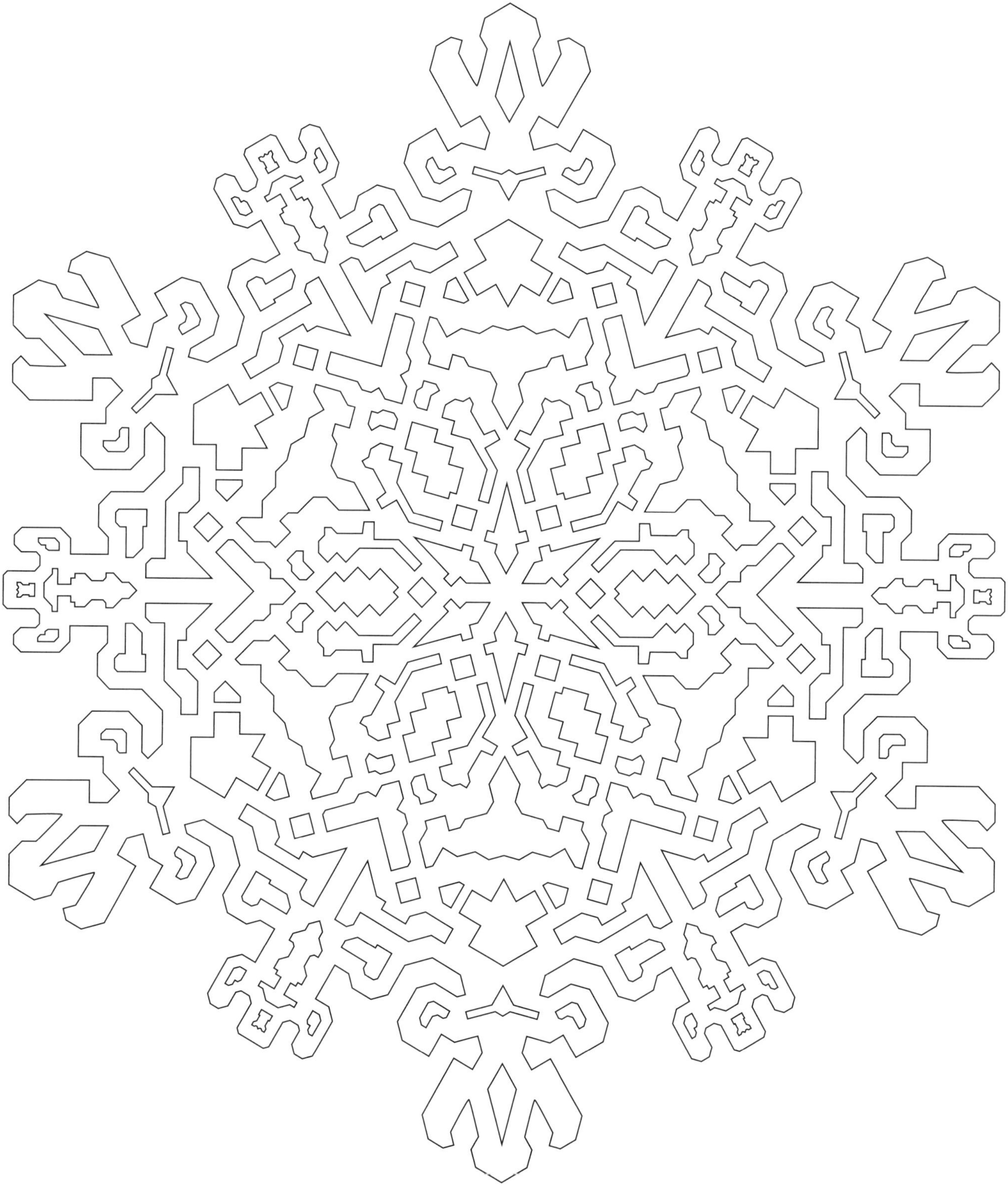

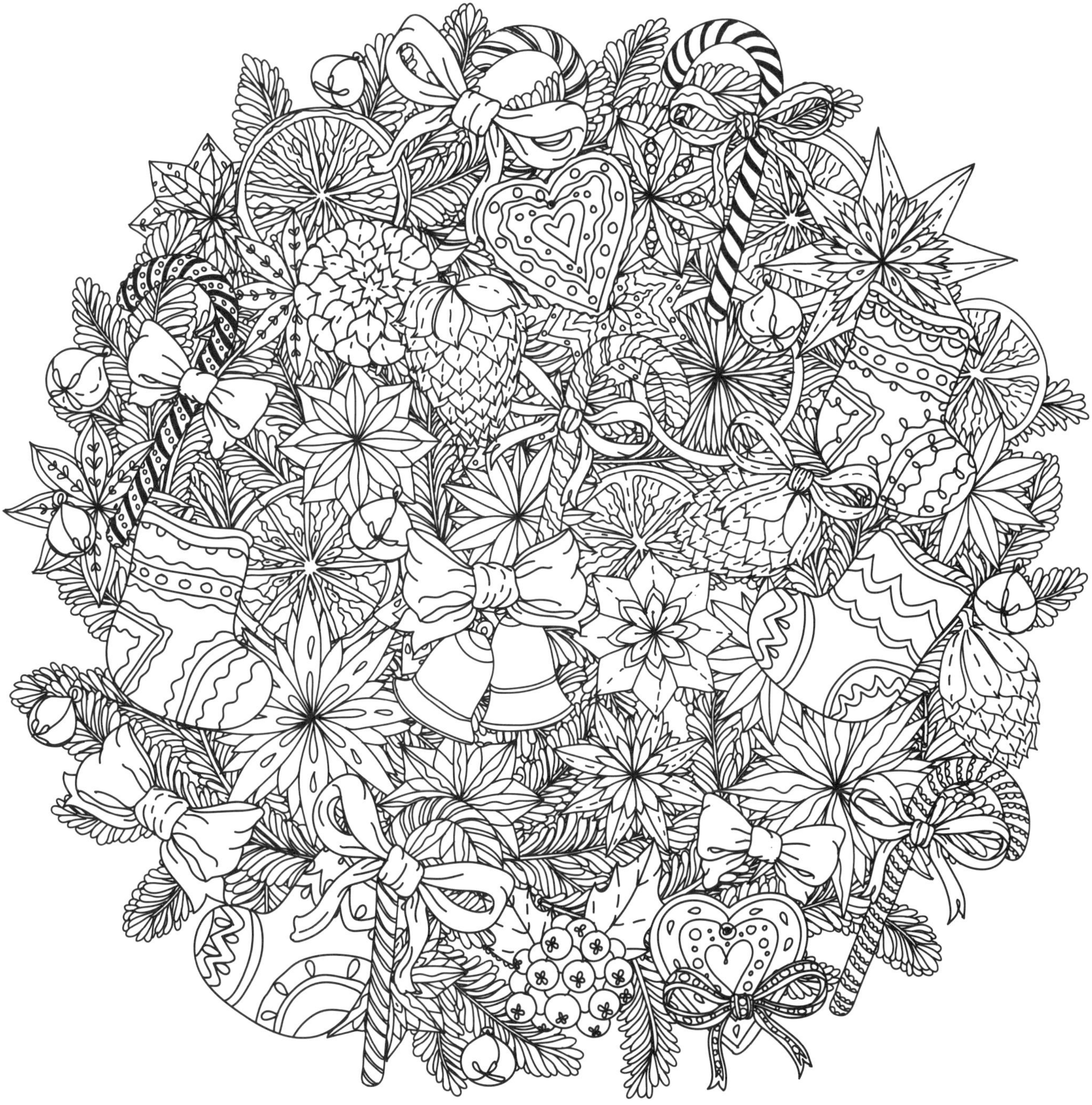

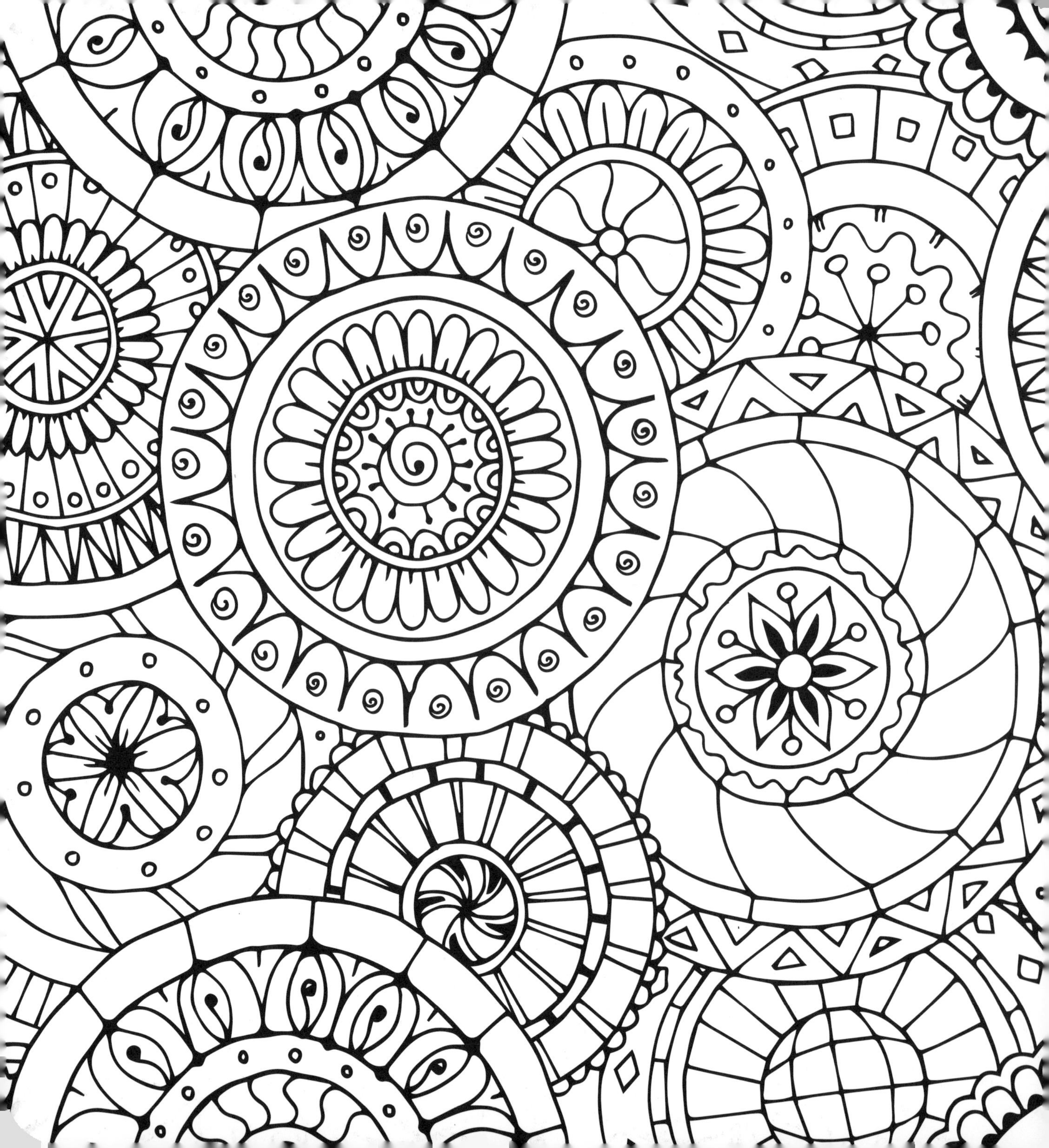

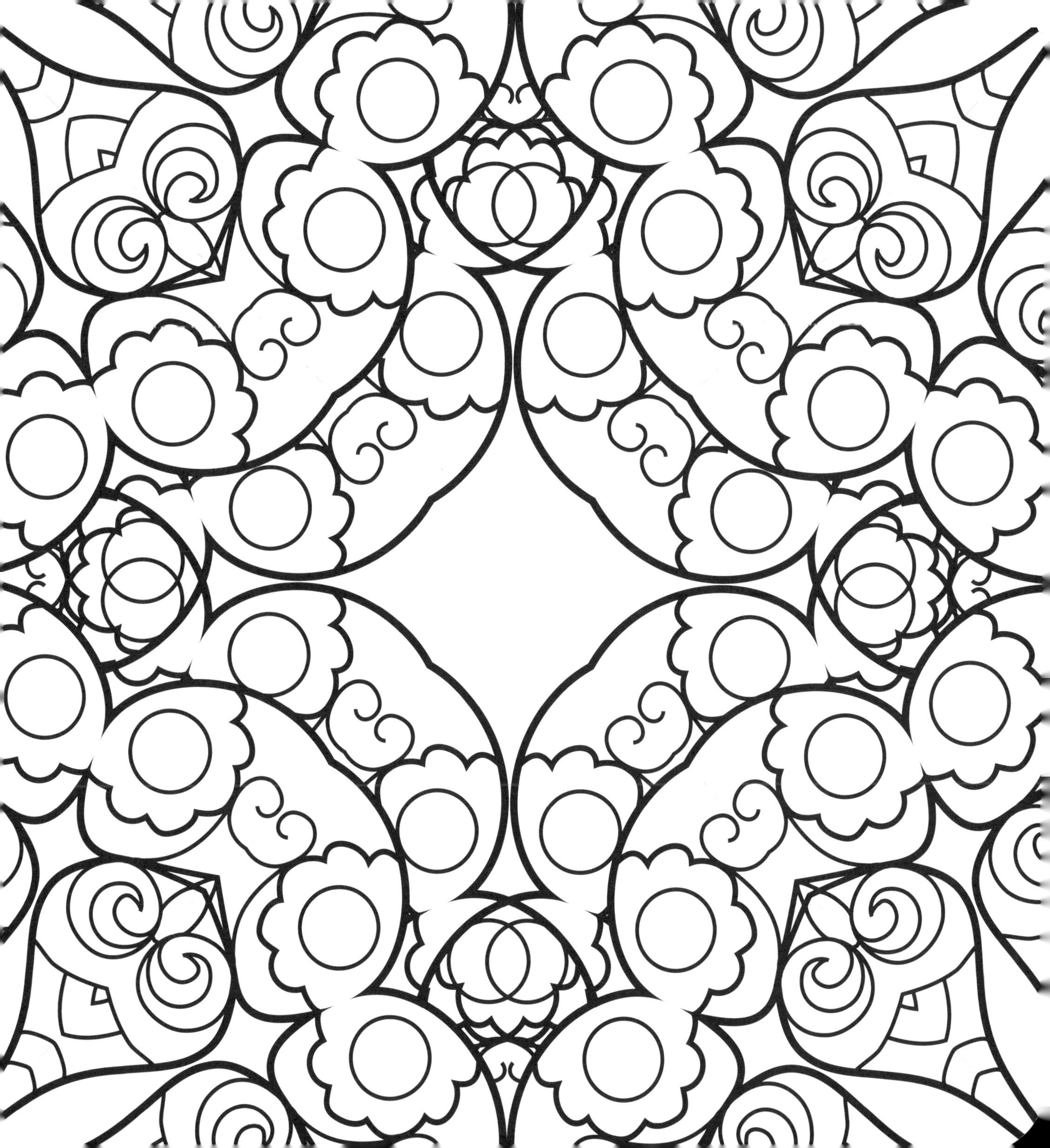

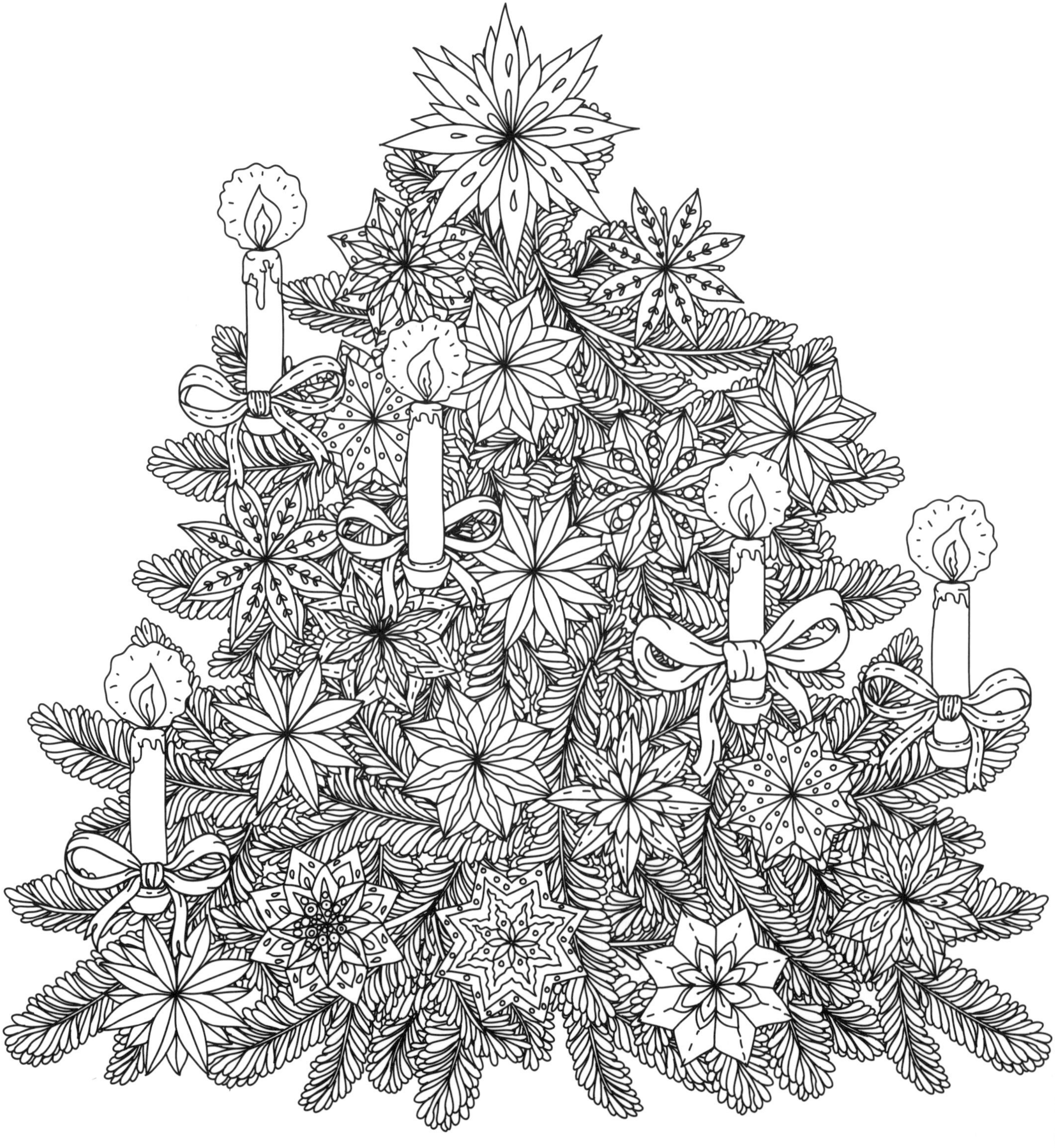

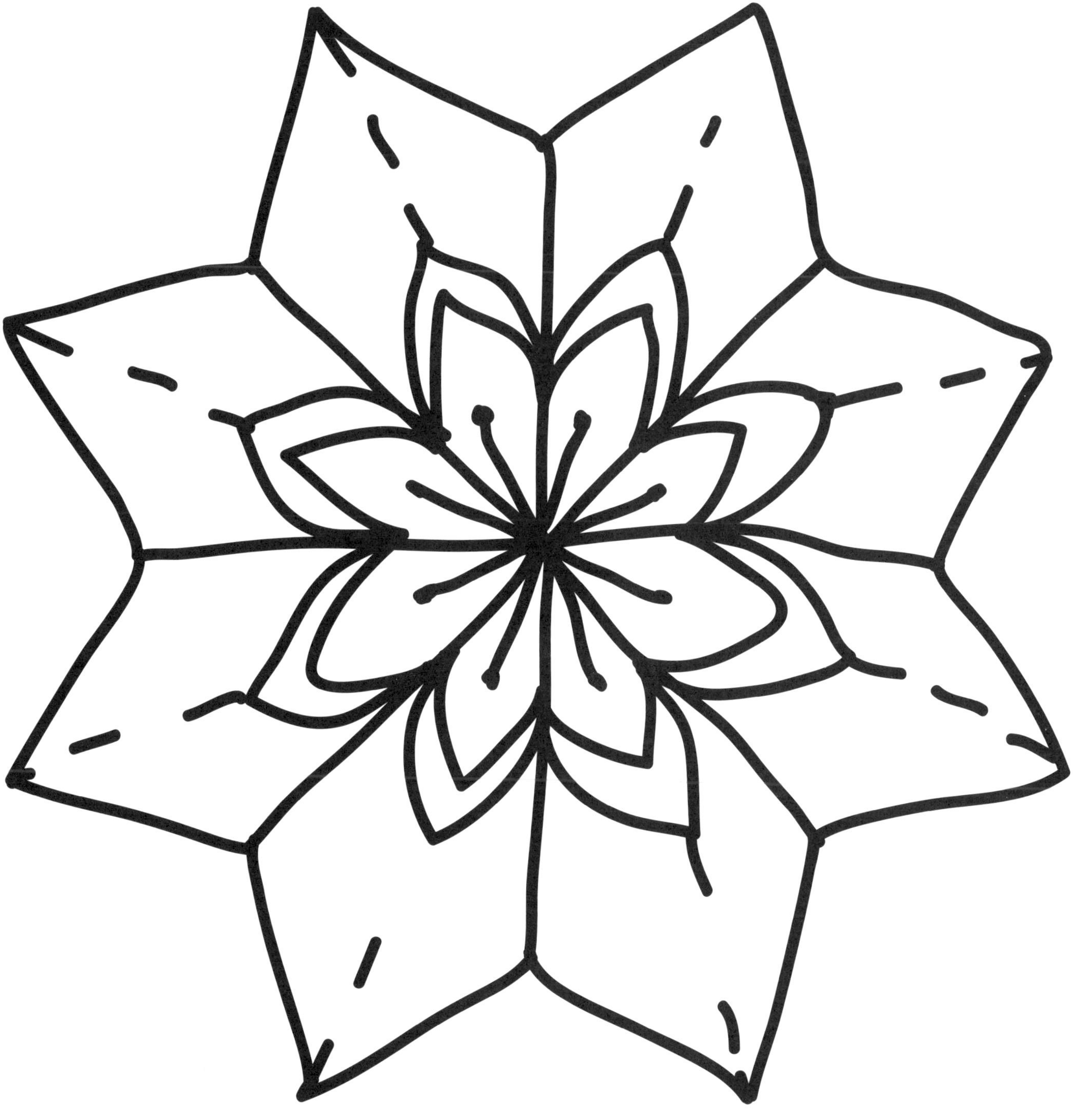

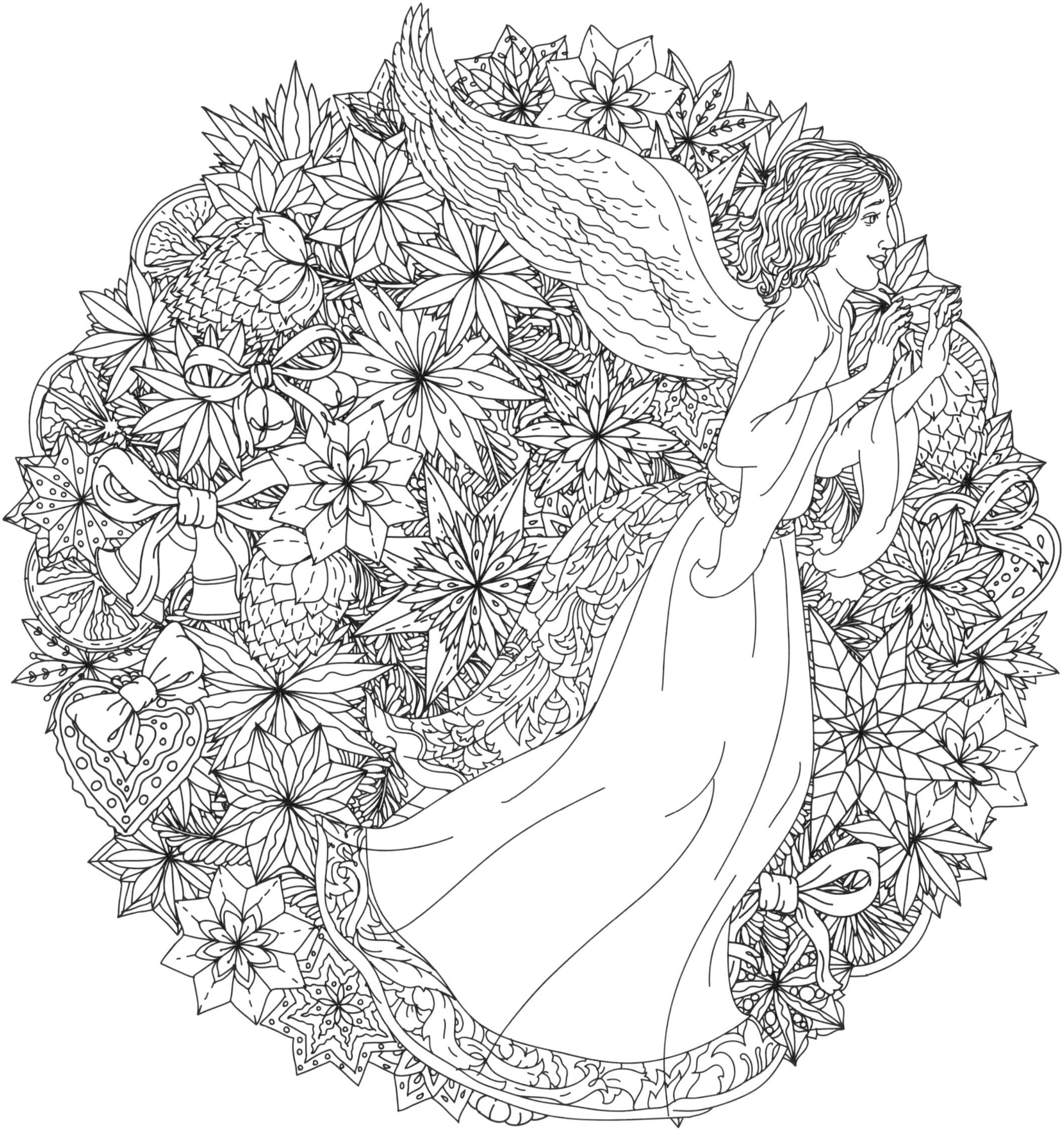

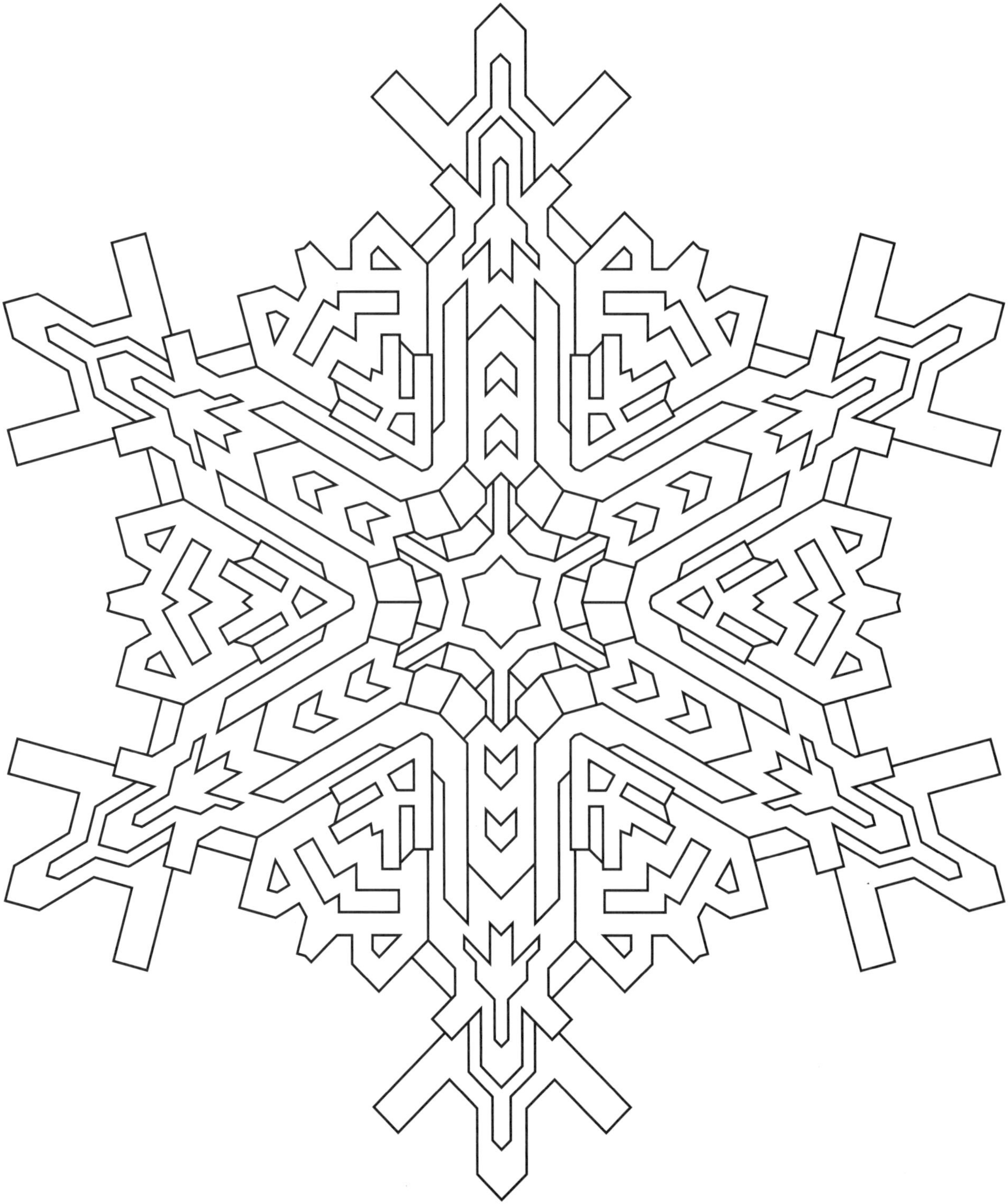

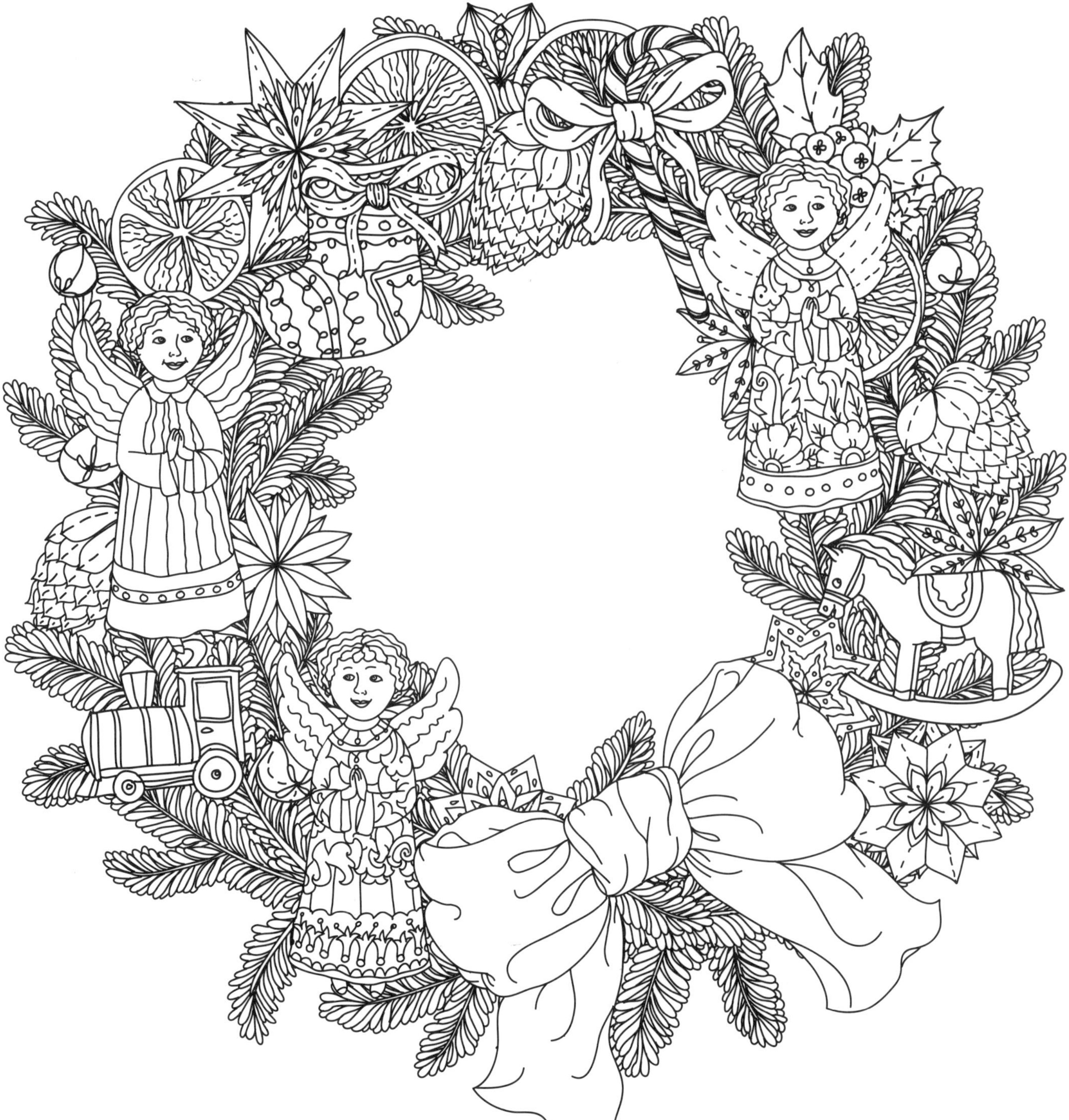

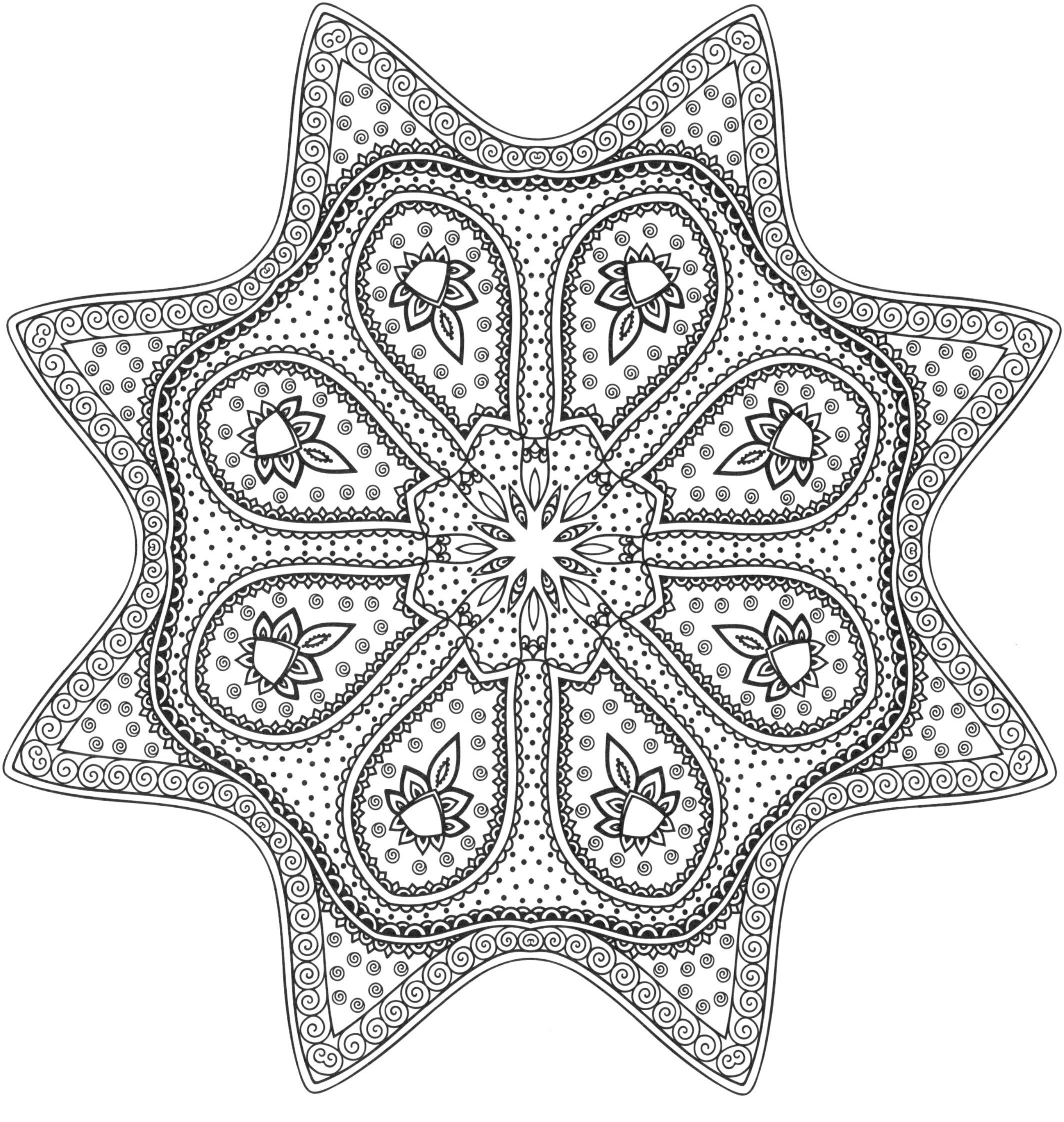

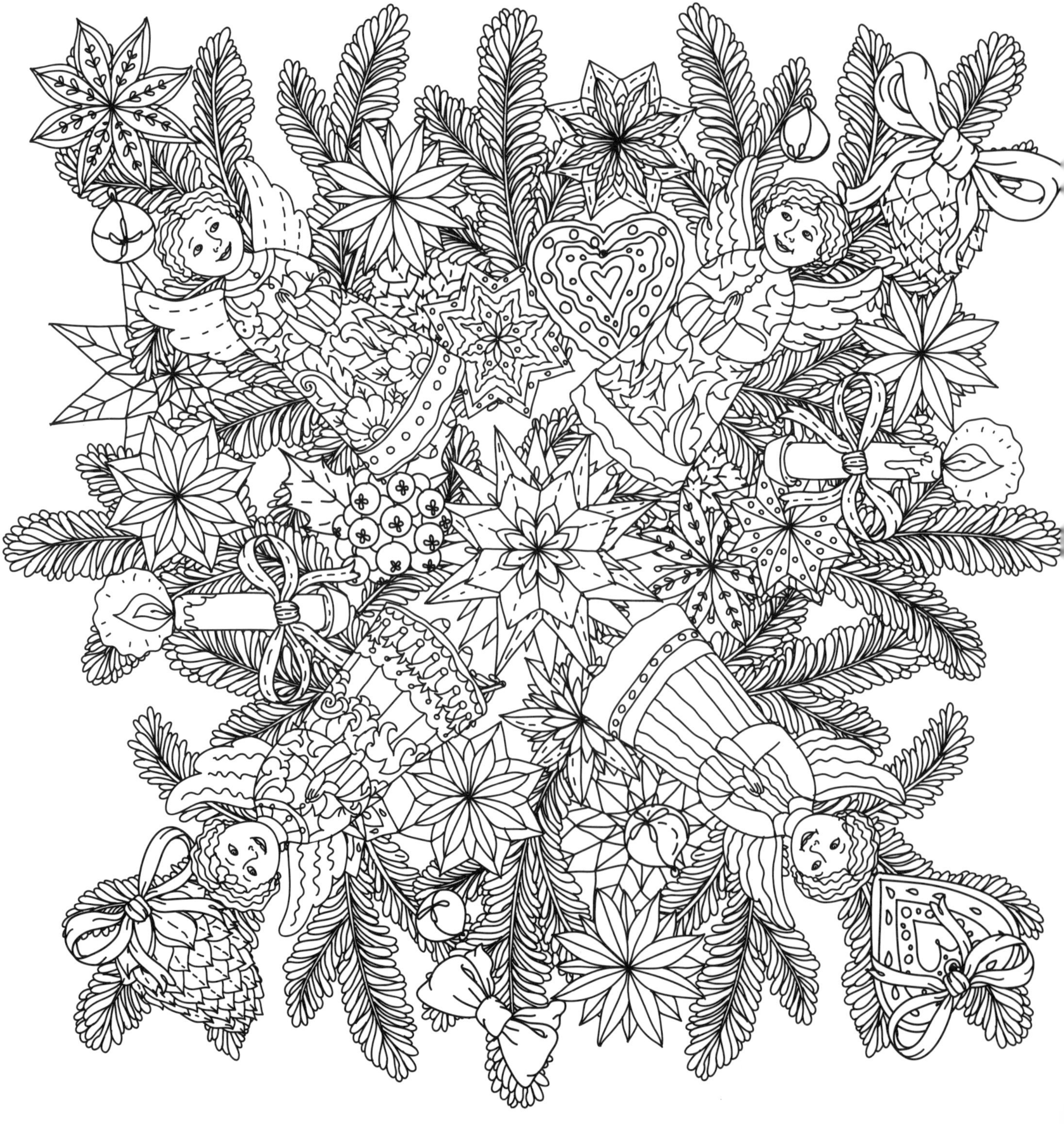

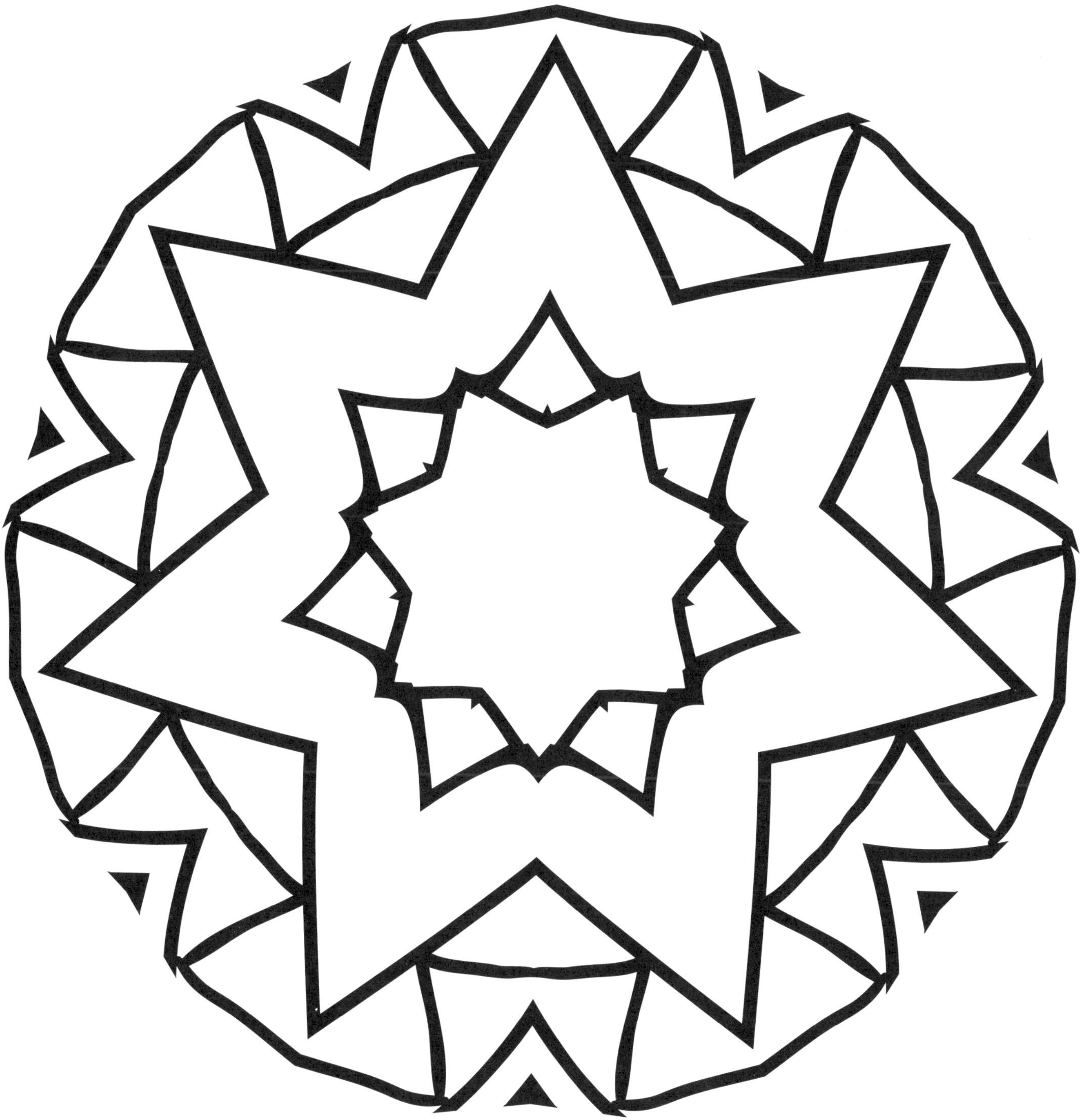

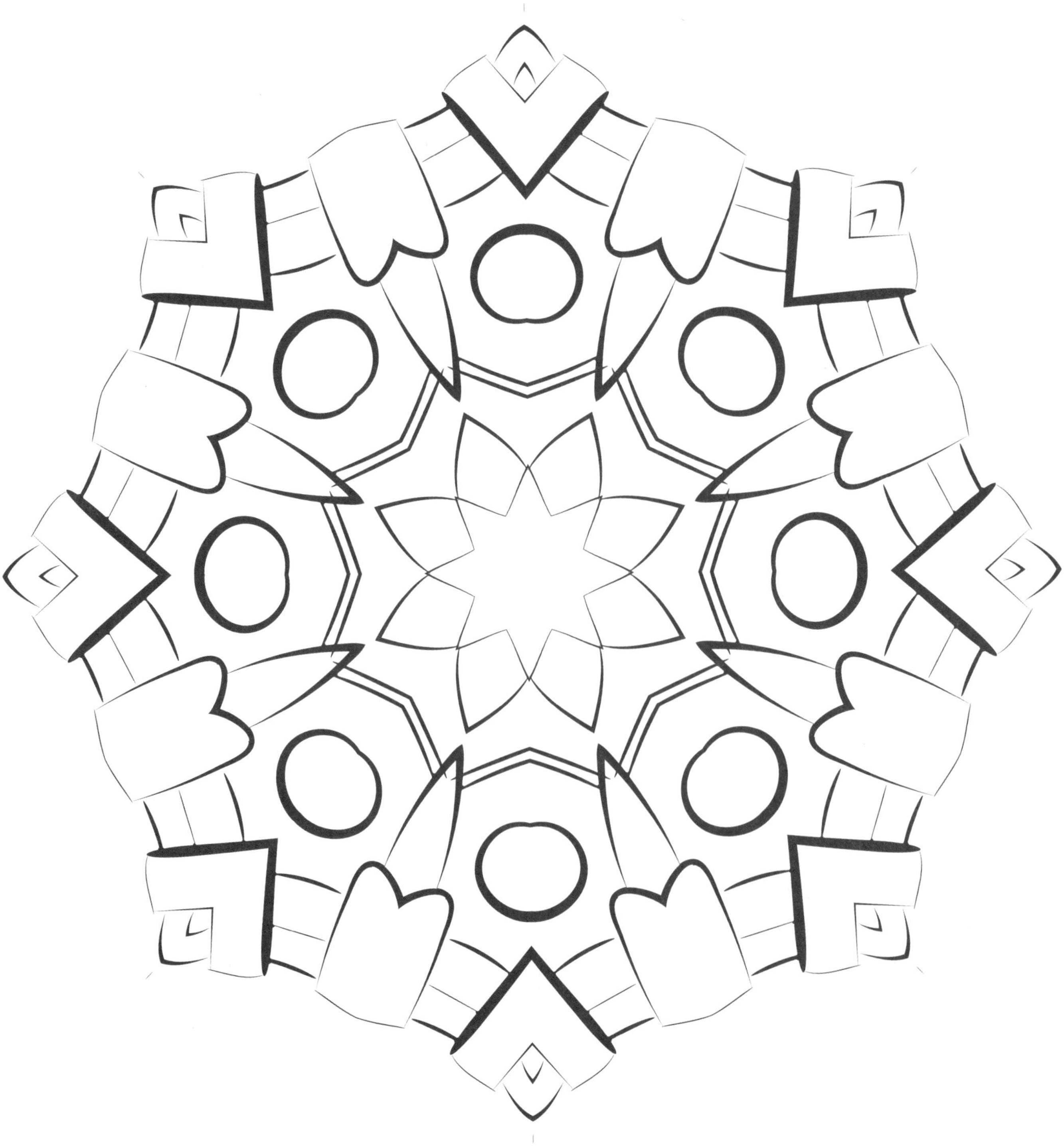